Improve Executive Functioning Skills Workbook For Kids

Activities To Strengthen Your Childs Working Memory, Develop Self-Control, And Become Organized At Home And School

Sibley Hall

Table Of Content

Introduction 1

Chapter 1: What Is Executive Functioning? 3

Chapter 2: You Are The Boss In Your Brain 8

Chapter 3: How Can You Help Your Youngster Develop Independence And Executive Functioning Abilities? 13

Chapter 4: Executive Functions: The "Big Ten" 19

Chapter 5 Activity 1: Self-Evaluation Of Executive Abilities 30

Conclusion 150

Resources 152

Introduction

If you're reading this, it's either because someone has told you that your kid has executive functioning issues or you've heard the term "executive functioning" thrown about in the education world and are curious about what it means. In any respect, you've come to the right place.

Firstly, the phrase executive functioning is a concept that suits the boardroom. That's presumably because the term executive conveys an idea of somebody completing all of the responsibilities necessary for achievement in a company – being organized, moving forwards when necessary, planning, and thinking about the future. Nevertheless, if you want your kid to grow up and become the next CEO of a big organization, this book is not for you. It is about training your kids to be the CEO who controls their learning.

Let's explore the definition of executive functioning. Children who struggle with executive functioning are frequently referred to as "dumb," "scatterbrained," "inconstant," or "losing." These troubles often manifest themselves as difficulties in the classroom, such as forgetting to hand in assignments, making thoughtless mistakes, and needing help staying on target and keeping up with the speed of the school. Youngsters may also have difficulties in their everyday life at home. They may misplace their stuff, have problems remembering their regular routines, forget to do their tasks, or have emotional responses that are disproportionate to the circumstances. Issues in executive functioning may also affect one's interpersonal connections.

Children possess a distinct assortment of talents and shortcomings. Each child has unique talents and weaknesses. Similar to how some kids pick up learning like something of a duck to the waters, confident kids pick up time-management skills, organization, preparation, and self-discipline through little direct teaching. These are the kids that excel at managing their time. On the other hand, some less dependable kids need more help in reading or other activities that demand executive functioning. They will need more extensive treatments to achieve the same degree of achievement as some peers. In this book, you will discover many tactics that work for children and adolescents struggling with executive functioning. Luckily, the book has theoretical and activity parts for parents that will help kids struggling with executive functioning and help their parents manage them.

Understanding that kids develop and learn at their special rates might help parents become more tolerant of difficult children. It is naturally irritating to have a kid who is continually leaving possessions around, neglecting to bring in an assignment you spent many hours assisting with, or delaying for an extended period. Remember that no kid wants to disappoint their parents and teachers by not meeting their standards. Sometimes the problem isn't with the child's drive; instead, they lack the skills and experience necessary to be productive. The purpose of this workbook is to assist you in trying and understanding the place to set the bar for your kid to master executive functioning abilities and establish practical techniques for educating them to attain that level. Let's begin!

Chapter 1: What Is Executive Functioning?

The term "executive functioning" is unfamiliar to most parents even when it can make a massive difference in the lives of children.

Children with executive functioning disorders are often characterized as "sluggish," "forgetful," "incompatible," or "lost." Their struggles frequently result in issues in the classroom, such as forgetting to turn in homework, making thoughtless mistakes, and struggling to stay on target and keep up with the class's pacing. However, a youngster could have difficulties at home, too. They could misplace their possessions, have problems memorizing routines, neglect their responsibilities, or exhibit emotionally inappropriate responses. Executive functioning issues impact social interactions as well. Friendships may suffer; youngsters can forget to meet up with their buddies, speak without thinking, misplace borrowed objects, or show impulsive behavior at social events. These issues are expected when the child lacks executive functioning, and the excellent news is that teaching these kids executive functioning skills is possible. Understanding what executive functioning and particular skills are required is the first step in supporting your kid in trouble.

Several technical descriptions of executive functioning are found in psychology. Most experts agree that executive functioning abilities encompass all the cognitive skills required to control your thoughts, feelings, and actions, often to achieve a goal.

It's crucial to understand that executive functioning abilities are also necessary for all other brain abilities, including remembering, concentration, motor function, verbalization, visualization, and finishing learning activities. Emotional regulation also makes use of executive functioning abilities. If we look at it another way, executive functioning is the operator of the brain, which is the engine of learning and self-regulation.

Extremely important

If your child's teacher or any professional dealing with your child mentions that your child has executive functioning issues, ask them to specify what particular traits are troublesome. Instead of all the administrative functions, a few organizational functioning abilities may need to be addressed. It will make it easier for you to create focused interventions to support your kid.

The following fundamental capabilities are often mentioned when defining executive functioning skills:

- **Task Launching:**

You are ending what you're doing and beginning something fresh.

- **Response Repression:**

It prevents impulsive behavior from accomplishing an objective.

- **Focus:**

You focus on a task while controlling distractions, directing your attention, and maintaining your concentration.

• **Time Administration:**

It is the process of knowing when time is passing, effectively using your time in advance, and avoiding procrastination.

• **Working-Memory:**

You are utilizing enough time to use your knowledge efficiently (remember it, process it, and act on it).

• **Flexibility:**

It is the process of adapting your plans and ideas to new circumstances.

• **Self-Regulation:**

You can reflect on your behavior and actions and make the necessary modifications to achieve a goal.

• **Emotional Restraint:**

You control your emotions and think about your sentiments to prevent impulsive conduct.

• **Task accomplishment:**

You are maintaining your levels of focus and effort to complete a task.

• **Organization:**

You are keeping count of, caring for and preserving order in your environment and your possessions (personal items, academic work).

Over the last twenty years, research on executive function has multiplied, frequently incorporating brain-based neurobiology. The prefrontal cortex, also known as the frontal lobe, is the part of the brain linked to administrative processes, including organization, planning, changing focus, problem-solving, and consciousness. Parents should be aware of the prefrontal cortex's continued development into emerging adulthood. One of the most critical parts of a child's development to reach maturity is their executive functions. As a result, you shouldn't anticipate that your school-age children and teenagers will possess completely mature executive functioning abilities. It is ongoing work to understand the administrative control center of the brain more efficiently. Understanding this helps make parents, instructors, and other adults more aware of children's needs who have difficulty in certain areas.

The most challenging test of executive functioning is becoming a parent

Consider how you utilize executive functioning in your own life to help understand how your kid uses these abilities. Parents are the heads of their households. They make Timetables, alter plans as needed, forego leisure pursuits in favor of raising their children, and prepare for the future. In reality, the abilities required to run your home are precisely the same executive functioning abilities you are probably working to instill in your kid.

For instance:

What do you do first when arranging a family vacation? Do you all get in the vehicle one morning and drive out on vacation without any itinerary, map, or clear instructions? Not if your family is impulsive and spontaneous! You may discuss your travel plans with your family, make decisions based on cost, climate, and availability, and examine everybody's calendars to find out when each person is available. Give pals close to your destination a call a few weeks beforehand and let them know you'd want to visit them.

Because you won't be returning from vacation with a massive backlog of work to accomplish, you may look into how to travel there by vehicle or aircraft, arrange for dog and house sitters, request that time off from work, and complete some job assignments beforehand. You might save aside cash for the vacation, put it on your credit card, and mentally plan how to pay it off later.

You may develop a list of the things you'll have to carry as the trip draws near an end and start packing a day or two beforehand. Executive functions include planning, organizing, forecasting, and foresight abilities. They serve as the mental route and schedule for completing a task. Whether you know them or not, you utilize them daily.

Chapter 2: You Are The Boss In Your Brain

Using visuals may aid when discussing executive functioning with kids. Ask your kid to imagine a little person at the forefront of the brain—the frontal lobe—as the person or thing in charge of it. The "boss" instructs them on what to focus on first, memorize it, and process other important information. Young people like having control over things! For a particular reason, telling a child that she gets to be the boss of designing her scientific project connects more with her than saying that she is "accountable" for doing so.

If your youngster needs to catch up in specific executive tasks, use the boss example to deepen your explanation. For instance, you may comment, "It feels like the boss in your head was taking a break!" if your youngster forgets to do some of his schoolwork. Let's review these instructions once again. It might be an excellent technique to gently inform kids and teenagers about their issues if they are responsive to input. It can also use the example to encourage your youngsters when they employ an executive function (e.g., "Wow! You spent twenty minutes just concentrating on your arithmetic task! Your brain's supervisor is working hard right now."

Practical Example

Imagery is a helpful tool when teaching youngsters complex topics like executive functioning. Look for a metaphor or picture that appeals to your youngsters, possibly one that reflects their hobbies.

If your kid likes trains, for instance, you may use a comparison "Like a train traveling up a steep track, it takes some effort to get started on your schoolwork, but that effort will help you do your work quickly and efficiently!"

"Boat Rockers" against "Smooth Sailors"

Every child develops and learns at varying rates. Some children pick things up quite quickly, while others need additional parental guidance. Consider reading skills as an example: Some kids start reading relatively young, often without much training. With the help of conventional reading assistance, some kids successfully acquire reading abilities. However, other kids need more detailed and specialized training, direction, and repetition before becoming proficient readers. The development of executive functions follows the same rule. Some kids quickly pick up the skills of self-control, self-monitoring, and independence.

What would development appear like for "smooth sailors" who quickly pick up on activities requiring executive functioning? These youngsters need recalls while learning anything new, but after a few repetitions, they get used to the pattern and require progressively fewer reminders.

They could also have creative problem-solving skills. They can emerge independently, without much adult direction, with a quicker, better, or unique solution to a problem when given a new assignment. They often resist distractions like TV, YouTube, Facebook, and outdoor games to do chores or projects.

Furthermore, even the most experienced sailors require adult assistance to learn how to accomplish tasks. They are good at remembering duties, doing homework, spotting errors in their studies, and planning for the future for large projects and exams. Smooth sailors efficiently turn off displays to concentrate on a project and communicate their emotions rather than acting out. They require less adult involvement than children who struggle with executive functioning. They have the propensity to adapt from their errors and store away techniques for more straightforward applications in the future.

The "boat rockers," meanwhile, are the opposite. Regardless of how often you remind them of anything, they always forget it. They are noted for their ups and downs patterns and working in surges. They remain on top of their job one week, suddenly lose things, become trapped, and start putting things off again the following week. When a new plan is suggested, they can become enthused, give it a go, lose interest, and revert to old, ineffectual tactics. They need help to control themselves, and their performance often leaves them unsatisfied. They typically wish to do superior yet feel they cannot do it. They sometimes quickly give up. They need a great deal of adult assistance to do chores that maybe their classmates or siblings can complete on their own.

Boat Rocker Parenting

Parents of "boat rockers" might struggle with them. Parents frequently find that their executive functioning-challenged kid needs additional common sense.

You may feel angry because it seems clear that your kid will remember to take a project to Monday's school after working on it the entire weekend. You're surprised it takes two hours to complete something that can be done in 10 minutes. Parents may need to remember how it feels to discover something new and challenging. Starting and focusing might be difficult for youngsters with executive functioning problems. Remember the last time you developed a brand-new skill or did something complex, like setting the DVR, mending a flat tire, learning a new computer program, or studying lengthy tax paperwork? This way, you will have greater empathy and patience with your kid, who is learning something new on a daily basis.

Learning anything new or challenging is annoying. Helping you through the process reduces frustration. You'll grow more frustrated if anybody orders you to finish in 10 minutes.

How would you describe when your youngster struggles with familiar chores or workouts? Why can't she recall the schedule? You may say, "I shouldn't be required to remind you to perform this task daily!" Even with everyday chores, your kid with executive functioning issues may struggle. Consider stopping cigarettes or exercising harder. Old habits are difficult to change. Even with knowledge, setbacks occur.

Executive functioning is like learning an entirely new recipe. First, you must follow the directions, collect the supplies, ensure you have the right equipment, have enough time, and precisely measure and sequence the processes. You may be faster next time, but you still need the recipe. You might recall the recipes the third time, but you must ensure that it was 1/2 teaspoon, not 1/2 tablespoon.

After several repetitions, you might have internalized the formula. You may even play with the recipes without destroying them. Your youngster might have to "cook the recipe" further than usual. She might need some additional detailed reminders (teaspoon versus tablespoon). Tell her that practice makes perfect. You may need to help her adjust habits or "recipes" and explain how they might be similar yet different. It teaches flexibility. Modeling, repetition, and consistency are the cornerstones of teaching your kid techniques for internalizing routines, such as making his bed, cleaning his room, completing his schoolwork, assembling items for school days, or remembering equipment for sports or activities on the weekend. Having your child out of the door early in the morning or even finishing schoolwork at a reasonable hour may become a daily survival mode for parents. Parents should take a step back and consider what skills they are teaching their children to become independent.

Chapter 3: How Can You Help Your Youngster Develop Independence And Executive Functioning Abilities?

Choosing which skills need improvement is the first step. Then, you may focus on developing those talents. Parents sometimes start too fast when attempting to improve their children's conduct. If you consider a change you want to make, like reducing weight, you might prefer to take small steps (e.g., buying skim milk instead of whole milk, walking fifteen minutes around the block on your lunch hour). Little adjustments may make significant improvements. You may start with the following to assist your youngsters in developing their executive functioning skills.

Becoming an excellent role model for your kid involves modeling. Children pick things up from you. Toddlers mimic anything their parents say and want to attempt everything they do, as their parents are well aware. They must be shown how to perform things, often with your narration of the procedure. Commanding children without demonstrating to them doesn't work well. However, all kids gain from modeling, not just toddlers. Even grownups gain from watching someone do a job well. Consider all the how-to videos available on the internet. Observing somebody else do something is often more straightforward than reading instructions or attempting it alone without assistance when learning to accomplish various things.

One of the most effective teaching methods, particularly with younger students, is modeling. Speaking aloud to yourself in your kid's presence might have seemed foolish.

Still, it's a terrific approach to show them that every one of us employs "self-talk" to control our behavior and that we are always deliberating before acting. The internal conversation that directs adolescents and children with executive functioning issues through activities and tasks is often absent. You can teach this essential self-talk technique to someone by displaying and modeling the actions they need to follow.

Repetition

The adage "Repetition is the mother of all learning" may have caught your attention. Adolescents and children who struggle with executive functioning need more repetition than those who do not. They frequently require repetitions of routine, reassurances about protocols, and more excellent explanations regarding how to divide challenging work into a logical chain of achievable activities.

Consistency

If repetition is the mother of all education, then consistency is likely the father of routines and norms. In general, regularity helps kids and teenagers perform better. Children and adolescents with executive functioning issues must be consistent since they often have trouble internalizing routines and adhering to rules and instructions. If the rules and procedures are constantly changing, it is much more difficult for people to remember them.

Regular Practices

Sequencing is one of the problems that kids and teenagers with executive functioning issues often exhibit. They may not necessarily follow a logical sequence of events. They frequently need to catch up on the broader picture or one stage in a series while being too focused on a bit of detail or phase.

They often fall victim to incentives to put off starting or finishing tasks along the road. Setting up frequent rehearsals for the routines your kids are experiencing trouble with can help them internalize the pattern. When youngsters internalize a performance, they become more effective and need less adult direction.

Treatment strategies to improve executive functioning

The disorganization of children with poor executive functioning, including individuals with ADHD, is greater than that of other children. They can take an abnormally long time to get ready or feel stressed when doing easy housework. Because adolescents often misplace documents or begin week-long tasks the night before they are due, schoolwork may become a nightmare.

Cognitive disorder experts have developed strategies to support the organizing abilities that a kid with weak executive functioning generally lacks. They impart various distinct techniques and alternate learning methods that support or strengthen a child's unique skills. They provide children—and parents—the following tools to help them manage their homework and other obligations that need planning and follow-through.

Checklists

Kids with executive dysfunction often need more awareness of the stages required to complete a job. Therefore, describing them in detail in advance renders a task less intimidating and more doable. Making choices with less mental and emotional stress is another benefit of using a checklist for youngsters with executive dysfunction.

According to educational therapist Ruth Lee, "These students frequently become so preoccupied with the decision-making procedure that they do not even begin the activity. Or, if they start, they keep resuming even though they've come up with a better method to do it. Kids may concentrate their mental attention on the tasks by using a checklist.

Lee points out that you can create a checklist for almost anything, including how to leave home on time every morning—which is often an everyday challenge for children with executive dysfunction. Making your bed, brushing your teeth, getting dressed, eating breakfast, grabbing your lunchbox, and getting your bag are some items on a checklist that some parents claim might save their sanity. Additionally, Lee advises doing the majority of the morning's duties the night prior. Children and parents can arrange clothes, prepare lunches in advance, and bags can be organized and awaiting at the entrance. She continues, "It requires a little additional forethought, but completing the job in advance may avert much turmoil the following day."

Limit your time

Many educational psychologists advise adding a time restriction to each stage when creating a checklist, especially if it is a more significant, longer-term assignment.

Children may practice breaking down several homework assignments to become familiar with the processes needed—and classify them based on how long these tasks could take.

Use the calendar

Education experts also stress the critical significance of adopting a planner. Nowadays, most schools mandate using planners, but they seldom instruct kids on how to utilize them properly. Therefore, it won't be apparent to a kid who is overwhelmed by—or disinterested in—planning and organization. It's sad because children having difficulties with executive functioning also have poor working memories, making it challenging to recall things like schoolwork. Problems with working memory often become worse at times. According to Dr. Cruger, "Children don't recall that if they don't write down their homework, they won't remember it. No matter how many times they forget, they pay no attention to it. As an alternative to coordinators, many schools now employ software tools like eChalk to build websites where instructors publish academic tasks and handouts, relieving the stress on children with executive dysfunction.

Describe the justification

A youngster acquiring new abilities must comprehend the reasoning behind using them for planning so that they don't seem like a waste of time or an unnecessary strain on energy. Children with poor organizing abilities often experience pressure from their obligations and duties and may be impatient when something is delayed. Dr. Cruger states, "it almost appears that they are generating neuroeconomic judgments." Planning might seem like a waste of time if they need to grasp its reasoning since they continuously evaluate if anything is worth their time.

Due to their more significant level of habituation, older children are more resistant. Even if their approach is ineffective, they will assert that it is what works for them, claims Dr. Cruger.

A youngster is considerably more likely to commit to using a particular method when its reasoning is explained.

Use incentives

Koffman advises implementing a reward system for younger children. "Younger children need external motivators to emphasize the importance of these new techniques. Kids may easily understand the relationship between honing their talents and working for a reward by using a tool like a star chart. Koffman adds that it's also an intelligent method to show children that their parents and teachers respect this talent. Hanging a reward chart in the designated homework area might be an excellent motivator if you're employing one. Parents should continue encouraging older children who are less motivated by awards and other incentives. Koffman advises parents to check in with older children.

"Check in on things or assist. Inform them that you value the hard work they've put in. Many children struggle in school. Therefore, they shouldn't assume that learning these things will be simple.

Chapter 4: Executive Functions: The "Big Ten"

It is better to consider executive functioning skills as an umbrella term that covers a wide range of abilities. These abilities are connected to the general knowledge of self-regulation, which is the capacity to keep track of, assess, and alter one's behavior with a purpose in mind. An analysis of the "Big Ten" executive functions will assist you in identifying the areas in which your kid may benefit from improvement. The following explanations of the abilities are checklists that will help you initially decide which sites to focus on for assistance. Consider your kids as executive dysfunctioned if they face any difficulties listed within any Big Ten executive functions. You may order your priorities according to which areas cause you or your kid the most stress or which have the most significant difficulties.

Task Initiation

Task initiation requires much energy to switch tasks. Executive functioning issues make it hard for kids to go from one study to another. Even adolescents (and adults!) lacking executive functioning skills may face these issues. Switching gears distinguish mild from severe problems beginning a new work. A typical youngster may complain and put off putting out the garbage, while a teenager may put off working until the last possible minute. These behaviors are consistent among children and teens with executive functioning issues. They could be habitual procrastinators who stay up late to do tasks they should have begun hours earlier, causing severe sleep deprivation. Task-initiation-challenged adolescents and children appear to lack the willpower to stop doing unwanted activities.

To establish how often your kid has trouble initiating tasks, ask yourself the following questions and mark any that apply.

- Have your youngsters ever struggled to start projects on their own?
- I need to figure out where to start! Is that something your youngster often says?
- Does your youngster typically need many cues and reminders to begin tasks?
- Does your youngster find it challenging to put down what he is doing and pick up something new?
- Do you consider your kid to be a "procrastinator"?
- If you ask your kid to undertake a task they don't really like, do they regularly object and pout?

If you tick three or more items, your kid may have task initiation issues and may benefit from treatments in this area.

1. Response Suppression

Response inhibition is when you talk yourself out of that beautiful slice of cake or avoid checking Facebook instead of drafting a report for work. Response inhibition prevents impulsive behavior from attaining an objective. Because of their limited attention span, young children have trouble deferring pleasure. Children learn to regulate their urges as they age and consider the repercussions. Because of a deadline, they may skip a baseball game with buddies.

When kids have much schoolwork, they may switch off their phones. They'll advise buddies to call back if they're working. Furthermore, adolescents and children with executive functioning impairments frequently acquire response-inhibition abilities later.

To determine your child's response-inhibition issues, ask yourself these things:

- From a very young age, my kid has always behaved impulsively.
- My youngster often "jumps first and thinks afterward," acting on the initial impulse.
- My youngster finds it very challenging to consider and adhere to "if-then" scenarios (e.g., If I finish my chores now, I can go play).
- I always tell my kid to put away screens (such as TV, phones, laptops, and tablets) so she can do her schoolwork.
- My kid makes casual errors in her work because she is impetuous.

If you ticked more than three questions, your kid might have response inhibition issues. You may intervene here.

2. Focus

Focusing helps kids learn and practice skills. Paying close attention is focusing on your work, ignoring distractions, and finishing it. Executive functioning issues may affect any of the following procedures in adolescents and children. Distractions vary. Some kids are inwardly preoccupied and daydream.

Everyone else is continuously diverted and will focus on anything around them—noises, people, things, etc. A youngster with attention issues may miss essential instructions while listening. Your youngster may have trouble focusing on schoolwork. Handling a distracted youngster may exhaust the most tolerant parent. However, teaching attention and distraction management may assist your kid in many aspects.

Use this checklist to analyze your child's attention issues:

- Does it appear that your kid isn't paying attention while you're giving directions?
- Does your kid struggle to complete one job, mainly if it demands patience and focus?
- Do you notice your youngster listening to background sounds while completing his homework?
- Does your youngster struggle to remain on the subject while speaking?
- Does your youngster grouse that it's difficult to focus?

If you selected three or perhaps more, your kid might need treatments to improve attention.

3. Time Management

Even grownups have trouble finishing their chores on time. Is it surprising that adolescents with executive functioning impairments, who struggle to create objectives, anticipate the future, and track time, also work with time management?

Adolescents, with increased responsibilities, extracurricular hobbies, and peer contact, have more obstacles. Procrastination and aversion may result from juggling "have to" and "would like to" chores. Time-management concerns may cause kids to be late, lose track of time, overestimate their abilities, or hurry to complete.

If your kid has time-management issues, use this checklist:

- Does your kid often forget the time?
- Does your kid often overestimate how long a project will take?
- Does your kid set ambitious standards for what he can do in a given time?
- Would your youngster lose appointments or planned activities without your reminders?
- Do you hear your kids complain about being short of time on examinations at school?
- Does your kid appear to have no sense of time passing?

If you selected three or all of these, you must plan time management treatments for your kid.

4. Working-Memory

Working memory is the ability to retain things in your head long enough to use them (remember them, process them, act on them). It controls how many files you may have open on your hard drive before your computer "crashes," analogous to RAM in your brain's computers.

Working memory is particularly crucial for learning since you need to recall information during the short term to retain it over a long time. Kids who need help with working memory frequently omit essential details from discussions, directions, and lectures, leaving gaps in their knowledge. They could also seem prone to forgetting whatever they are doing during the middle of it.

Choose which of the following is true for your kid using the checklist:

- My youngster has trouble following instructions that have several parts.
- For my kid to comprehend what she has read, she must reread it.
- If my kid doesn't note things down, like his schoolwork, he will forget them.
- Mental calculations are challenging for my youngster.
- My youngster has trouble doing many tasks at once.

If you ticked out three or more boxes, working memory could be an area that needs development.

5. Flexibility

Flexibility is the ability to adjust to changing situations. Children who have difficulty with mental agility (also called cognitive flexibility) tend to become "stuck" on an ineffective solution to a problem. They could also fixate on a troublesome detail and miss the larger picture. Academic problem-solving requires mental agility.

Students are expected to learn via abstractions as the difficulty of their curriculum increases. It means using what they know in novel contexts. Lacking flexibility, children struggle when a problem is somewhat different or when they must synthesize what they know to tackle a new challenge.

Social problem-solving requires mental flexibility. Situations change social norms. In the classroom and on the playground, your voice's loudness fluctuates. Your cheerfulness and self-disclosure rely on your audience and location. You must interpret social signs in real-time to determine whether someone is no longer listening or has been insulted. Changes in social contexts need adaptability. More "unwritten" regulations apply to older children.

How can you tell if your kid has cognitive flexibility issues? Mark the following behaviors that you have seen in your kid using the checklist:

- My youngster becomes "stuck" on one approach to problem-solving.
- Even though his homework method is inefficient, my kid may sometimes claim it is the best.
- My youngster sometimes thinks in "black and white" and fails to see the nuances of grey while addressing problems.
- My youngster struggles to comprehend unwritten social standards and adjust to new social circumstances.
- When engaging with other kids, my child occasionally appears to have a "my way or the highway" attitude.

You can start your treatments here if you agree with three or more cognitive flexibility difficulties.

6. Self-Regulation

Self-regulation involves reflecting on your activities and making adjustments to achieve a goal. Self-regulated learning is a multi-step process. Self-regulated kids use metacognition or understanding their thinking because they actively consider learning. They create objectives, construct a strategy, carry out the plan, monitor its progress, make modifications, if necessary, examine their performance, and keep mental notes around what works and what doesn't, then assess and self-reflect upon completing the activity. These abilities are continuously developing.

Therefore, we expect the youngster to refrain from going through them consciously. Academic self-regulation begins in the toddler years. Teachers and parents may demonstrate and educate self-regulation.

Does your youngster have trouble self-regulating? If your kid exhibits any of these behaviors, self-regulation may be a problem to address:

- My kid doesn't seem to have academic objectives that he sets for himself.
- It's difficult for my kid to recognize when she will not comprehend a learning job.
- My youngster doesn't seem aware of his learning skills and shortcomings.
- My kid seldom ever prepares a study schedule for an examination or a lengthy assignment.
- Despite often making errors in her work, my youngster does not appear to notice.

If your kid has three or more troublesome behaviors, you may want to intervene to teach self-regulation.

7. Emotional Self-Control

Emotional self-control is monitoring and reflecting on your emotions to avoid impulsive conduct. Emotional self-control requires awareness, labeling emotions (e.g., sad, annoyed, angry, thrilled), and managing reactions without behaving impulsively. Children that have trouble managing their feelings may strike, say unpleasant things, or act aggressively. Emotional kids don't always act out. Some kids have difficulty letting go of upset emotions and worry. While all adolescents struggle with expressing and comprehending emotions, those with executive functioning issues may have more problems. To determine whether emotional regulation needs assistance, check out the following statements for your child:

- My kid is a very emotional person.
- My child's emotions fluctuate a lot.
- When agitated, my kid has never been easy to calm down.
- Both adults and peers find it easy to disagree with or quarrel with my kid.
- My kid has intense emotional responses when corrected.

If you picked three or more boxes, you should focus your intervention on emotional self-control.

8. Task accomplishment

Seeing a job through to its conclusion while maintaining sufficient attention and energy is known as task completion. Task completion issues might arise at school and home; You could see incomplete or subpar work on activities around the house. Your kid may require much additional prodding to complete the things she began. Children with executive functioning issues often struggle to see activities through to completion, even when they are pleasurable jobs, projects, or interests. These issues may arise in assignment completion. Homework demands a mental "stick-to-it approach" Some kids develop tenacity later. Complex issues cause kids to abandon schoolwork. It's seldom just motivation. Occasionally kids are confused or overwhelmed and don't know where to begin. They start but quit when they get trapped. When the work is too hard, the youngster avoids and dislikes it. On the other hand, only some jobs may bore children. You may need to work with your child's teacher(s) and at home to find the cause of their homework problems.

Is your youngster having trouble finishing tasks? Check the boxes next to the statements that apply to help you discover areas where your kid could have difficulties using this checklist:

- When performing tasks, my youngster becomes distracted and only completes them partly or slowly.
- It takes a lot of cues and reminders to get my kid to do their schoolwork.
- My kid won't do her schoolwork if I don't sit next to her.
- My youngster only appears to put some effort into activities he enjoys.
- My child's teachers complain that she doesn't complete her work in class.
- My youngster quickly gives up on schoolwork.

You could concentrate your treatments on task completion if you identified three or more problems for your kid.

9. Organization

Organization entails maintaining a record of your possessions (personal and academic) and organizing your own space. Executive functioning deficits make organization challenging for kids. Their bedrooms are typically dirty, their bags full of shredded papers, their tables full of strange objects, their notebooks disheveled, and they serve as "regular fliers" found at their campuses! Parents and instructors frequently don't comprehend why children with organizational issues can't "get it together."

Despite the most outstanding efforts, kids often fail to meet adult standards. They may feel ashamed. Adults can assist children in organizing, but they must learn how to arrange themselves.

- Does your youngster have organizational issues?
- My kid seems to make a mess everywhere she goes.
- My kid often misplaces items, including coats, lunchboxes, schoolwork, books, and critical documents.
- Even after I explain where things should go, my youngster still doesn't know where to place items.
- My kid regularly forgets to bring notebooks, textbooks, or papers home.
- My child's workstation is unorganized and unkempt.

If your kid has difficulties in three or more areas, you should teach them organizing skills as a top priority.

Chapter 5 Activity 1: Self-Evaluation Of Executive Abilities

For your knowledge

Kids with executive function disorder (EFD) struggle to accomplish particular activities necessary to carry out their everyday obligations. These comprise but aren't limited to planning, organization, and analysis. Kids with EFD may struggle in the classroom to complete and turn in assignments on time, maintain order in their lockers, notebooks, and binders, and manage their time while avoiding distractions. Children with EFD can struggle at home to control their emotions, follow instructions, or keep their rooms tidy.

Some individuals have superior executive abilities than others, just like the height differences, as some kids are short and some are tall. If you have EFD, you are not "abnormal"; instead, you are simply a bit different from the standard. It could be preferable to use the word "average" rather than "normal." You may conceive most kids as having average brains.

You may learn your executive functioning strengths and weaknesses by taking the following exam. After working on your weaker regions, move on to the areas that only need a little focus. Your productivity will increase as your executive talents improve.

Your Tasks

Please read the following sentences carefully.

Circle those that apply to you based on what you know about yourself or have been told by others.

Area 1:

- I do activities quickly and finish them on time.
- I prefer to avoid activities or video games that need the use of problem-solving techniques.
- I want the instructions to be repeated several times.
- I've been accused of being ignorant of how my actions affect others.

Area 2:

- I often need to pay more attention to bringing home the supplies I need to finish my tasks.
- I need help finding my finished tasks in my logbook.
- I need help keeping my room, bag, locker, or work neat and organized.
- I often need help locating things that I need.

Area 3:

- It is challenging for me to get started on tasks early enough to finish them on time.
- I need help to accommodate new programs into my calendar.
- It is difficult to predict how long it will take to finish a task.
- I frequently miss deadlines or due dates for assignments or projects.

Area 4:

- I often throw rage tantrums.
- I experience anxiety more frequently than other children of my age.
- I find it difficult to control my anger.
- I get annoyed about little things.

Area 5:

- I cut off discussions.
- Most people have complained to me that I say or do nasty things.
- I begin projects without waiting or thoroughly reading the directions.
- I speak out of turn in the classroom, even without the instructor calling on me.

Area 6:

- I find it challenging to adapt to unforeseen changes in a timetable.
- I need help moving from one class to another or going from campus to home at the end of the day.
- I give up if I don't succeed at anything on my first try.
- I find it difficult to ask for assistance when something needs to be clarified.

Area 7:

- It is challenging to begin projects on my own.
- I need help to complete obligations like housework and assignments.
- It is hard for me to obey home or classroom norms.

- It is challenging to switch between tasks.

Area 8:

- I need help to finish projects, particularly if they get challenging.
- I feel overburdened by significant tasks or initiatives.
- It is challenging to ignore external disturbances when doing homework.
- I converse with others around me rather than concentrate on a task.

Area 9:

- I find it challenging to recall spoken lists of three or more items.
- I need to turn in all of my schoolwork.
- I often forget to bring home the supplies I need to finish my task.
- I only respond to the first section of a query with numerous parts.

Area 10:

- If I'm distracted while working on anything, it's difficult for me to pick it back up.
- If the work is tedious, I have difficulty keeping "on track."
- While attempting to concentrate on my task, I am easily distracted.
- I need help to create objectives at home or in school.

If you pick two of four items, you need to be stronger in that domain of executive functioning. Exercises in this workbook can assist you in honing your talents in each of the following areas:

Area 1: Self-Awareness

(The capacity to judge how well you comprehend who you are and how you behave)

Area 2: Organizational Skills

(The capacities to create, preserve, and keep a record of objects):

Area 3: Capacity for Time Management

(The ability to utilize effective use of time and correctly predict how long an activity will take)

Area 4: Managing Emotions

(The capacity to remain composed in the face of circumstances that could otherwise make you feel agitated, furious, unhappy, or disappointed)

Area 5: Behavior Management

(The capacity to restrain oneself from misbehaving)

Area 6: Flexibility

(The capacity to alter your routine or habit)

Area 7: Initiative

(The capacity to begin undertakings or activities on your initiative)

Area 8: Pay Attention

(The capacity to maintain concentration when facing distractions while performing a tedious activity)

Area 9: Working memory

(The capacity to remember specific details to finish a job)

Area 10: Persistence

(The capacity to do tedious work without giving up)

Added tasks

Knowing where to begin when trying to improve your executive abilities might take much work. Setting aside time to sketch up a strategy for utilizing this book could be beneficial.

You might have discovered that you scored lower than average in several areas of executive functioning when you completed the evaluation on the preceding pages. Sort the findings of your assessment into the most outstanding and weakest categories. In other words, note any instances where you checked all four claims, then checked three, and so forth. After that, begin working on the tasks listed for activity one and move on to number ten.

1...

2...

3. ....

4. ....

5. ....

6. ....

7. ....

8. ....

9. ....

10.

....

Activity 2: Observing Oneself

For You to Know

One of the more challenging aspects of executive functioning deficiency is that, if you experience it, you may only sometimes be able to notice it. Occasionally you require other people to act as a mirror for you, reflecting any issues they perceive that you are experiencing. Identifying the problem might be among the most crucial aspects of developing a solution.

Jamal, who was fourteen, didn't get why his elder peers were constantly pursuing him. His parents and teachers always yelled at him. Jamal said that he performed well in school. He always participated in class. But he could not see that he was not giving his homework and duties his best effort, which was an issue.

Jamal's parents sat him down one day and tried to communicate their worries. According to them, he was a clever youngster but performing way below his potential. They advised him to get his act together, do better in class, and complete his responsibilities. Jamal initially refused to accept the "image" his parents were trying to paint for him. Over the next several days, he suspected that his parents were correct. He saw that his professors regarded him separately from the pupils, who were more adept at adhering to instructions and submitting their assignments on time.

Jamal decided to do a quick test. He worked hard the next three days to do his assignment and send it in. He put much effort into focusing during class and avoiding outside interruptions. After listening to his parent's instructions, he carefully noted what he was required to accomplish.

He immediately became aware of a change in how the grownups were treating him. They were more compassionate about his situation and prepared to spend time explaining these things to him. Jamal thus put more effort into these activities till they become habits.

Your tasks

Use words or images to express yourself in the top section of the below-following box. Also, include your strengths and weaknesses. Use pictures or words to communicate how your family, instructors, siblings, and friends view you in the section at the bottom of this box.

Include both positive and negative comments.

My View of Myself

____

____

____

____

The Way Others Look At Me

____

____

____

____

Added tasks

Respond to the following questions regarding what you wrote or sketched in the last activity.

How closely do you describe or view yourself to match how others tell or see you?

____

____

____

____

Does the way you describe or see yourself vary from how others describe or visualize you?

____

____

____

____

____

____

____

____

What do you suppose the causes of these variations are?

____

____

____

____

Which characterization or image do you believe is closest to the "actual" you? (Circle the response.)

My View of Myself **The Way Others View Me**

How could you begin reimagining "you" to make you better at accomplishing what you need to do and be the person others want you to be? How can you combine the positive aspects of both descriptions or images (or modify the negative aspects)?

Activity 3: Motion Is Sluggish

You must know

Children that struggle with executive functioning most often don't consider giving their work their best effort. Many people will do jobs quickly only to get them done. You can invest more effort into your actions if you can slow down.

Johanna, a twelve-year-old student, would rush over assignments and commit careless errors. She finished household duties so rapidly that they could have been completed to a higher standard. Johanna was unaware that her parents were upset by her conduct. She assumed everything was going OK.

Johanna's professors and parents finally decided to sit down with her after she got many failing grades. They described how they witnessed her racing to complete tasks and made the suggestion that this had a significant role in how effectively she finished her homework and other duties.

After acknowledging that these tasks could be correct, Johanna made a concerted effort to slow down. She discovered that she performed far better when she took her time with just about any work.

Her professors were pleased with the work Johanna submitted, and her parents were delighted with how Johanna completed her responsibilities. Johanna was happy that her family and instructors were satisfied, and she was pleased with the advancement of her marks.

For you to do

You can use the acronym/acrostic SLOW to help yourself remember to go slowly and methodically while working on a particular task.

S—Stop.

L—Listen to advice attentively.

O—Observe a person perform the work properly.

W—Work very hard to execute the work as directed.

Classify a few of the chores you often do too fast in the following chart.

Things that others have informed me I do too quickly	Things that others have informed me I do too quickly
At my School	**At my Home**
English spelling Test	Dishwashing

Consider which of the chores you outlined might benefit from SLOW usage. When are you able to take advice and imitate someone else's behavior?

Added tasks

Select a regular activity from the list you made in the last exercise, and then describe it in the following blank.

Next time you complete this work, calculate how long it requires you by performing it as usual while noting your beginning and ending times.
Time of start: ....Time of completion: ....How much time it took:.....................

On a scale of 1 to 10, rate how well you performed the job (1 being poor and ten being excellent). Mark it with a circle.

1 2 3 4 5 6 7 8 9 10

Use the same scale to grade your performance on the assignment by your parent or instructor. Mark the rating given by your parent or instructor.

1 2 3 4 5 6 7 8 9 10

Talk to your parent or instructor about how you may have performed the activity more effectively. List the ideas of the individual.

When you do the work again, make a note of the same beginning time. As you go, consider SLOWING down and focusing on the places where you may progress as a result of your conversation. Make a note of your completion time when you're done.

Time of start:........................ Time of completion:................How much time it took:..................

On a scale from 1 to 10, rate how well you performed the job (1 being low and ten being excellent). Mark it with a circle.

1 2 3 4 5 6 7 8 9 10

Use the same scale to grade your performance on the assignment by your parent or instructor. Mark the rating given by your parent or instructor.

1 2 3 4 5 6 7 8 9 10

Did it take you more time the second time to complete the task?

Where did your evaluations go, as well as those of your parents or teachers? (Circle the response.)

Improved, remained unchanged, became worse.

Activity 4: Recognizing Disarray

For you to know

Keeping your belongings in places where you can find them quickly and easily can help you be more productive in your everyday tasks. Being organized at home can lessen the likelihood that you or your parents will get frustrated while trying to locate lost belongings. Being collected at school will assist you in obtaining higher marks. The first step in honing this ability is to become conscious of how disarray impacts your life.

It's a moment to go to school, Bryce. His dad yelled at him from the basement. Bryce, a fifteen-year-old, began to fumble. He hurried down the stairs after grabbing his bag and putting on his shoes but turned around when he realized he had left his English class assignment behind. When the bus arrived, just as he was ready to board, he stuffed the paper into his bag, grabbed his jacket off the floor, and dashed out the door.

He sat down and muttered, "Whew, I made it." Then he realized he had left his lunchbox on the kitchen countertop. Dang, he exclaimed. He took out his phone and called his mother. Would you please bring my lunchbox to school?

His mom moaned. "Bryce, how many times do we need to encounter this? You forget your lunchbox one day and a textbook the next. You have to arrange yourself better!"

Mr. Stangl instructed the pupils in calculus class to bring their previous day's homework. Bryce combed through all of his files and bag. 'I'm sure I completed it,' Bryce remarked as Mr. Stangl paused at his desk. I left it on my writing table in my bedroom. I'll take it in tomorrow's class, I swear.

Bryce, submitting the work tomorrow is OK. However, you'll receive reduced marks since it is past due. When Bryce returned home, he made a mental point to include the math homework in his bag. Mr. Thompson instructed the student in chemistry class to prepare pencils for the exam.

"Oh, no!" Bryce yelled. "I was unaware that there is a test," His lab companion reminded him, "Yeah, the teacher told us about it yesterday." With a groan, Bryce pulled out a pencil. He had not even spent any time

studying. Therefore, Bryce only knew a portion of the test's answers. He reasoned that Mr. Thompson would let him repeat the exam.

Bryce arrived home after school, threw his bag on the dining room floor, pulled off his boots, retrieved a meal from the fridge, and then sat quietly in front of the Television. He watched TV for an hour before playing video games.

Your task

See if you can identify Bryce's erratic actions. Kindly list the activities in the below-mentioned chart that Bryce did or did not do to make his day busier. Then list the unfortunate events that occurred as a result of his disorder. For instance, the first one has already been completed for you.

Unorganized behavior displayed by Bryce in the story.	How this conduct harmed Bryce (There might be more than one effect)
Not possessing any assignments in the bag	Hurrying to get on the bus Reduced Grades

Added tasks

Complete the following chart with examples from your own life; sometimes, the harmful effects of your disorderly actions are not immediately apparent. Please consider all aspects of your life carefully.

Disorderly attitude in my life	How this conduct makes me feel uncomfortable
Example: A sloppy backpack	I could not locate my homework, which is why my marks suffered.

Activity 5: Perfect Sweep

For your understanding

Regularly sifting through your possessions and removing unnecessary or undesired items is a significant component of organized life. You would quickly find yourself drowning in a sea of guardianship if you kept everything you ever got! You may become more organized and make it easier to locate the items you require by regularly getting rid of stuff you don't need.

Like many other girls of her age, Tatiana, 13, kept her room in complete disarray. Her desk was covered in paper sheets, and her carpet with clothing. Many unfinished water bottles and snack wrappers were on her shelf because the clutter didn't bother Tatiana. She vowed that she wouldn't tidy her room since Tatiana could locate whatever she wanted.

The condition of Tatiana's bag was much the same. It was completely covered with papers from all sides. The documents were thrown into whatever folder she could find, making it impossible to locate the ones she wanted. Her academics were deteriorating as a result of this.

Tatiana's mother begged her daily to tidy up her bedroom and school bag. Tatiana would enter her bedroom intending to tidy it, but she would either get sidetracked by something she saw or be interrupted by a friend. She never seemed to have her room or bag organized.

Your task

Choose one part of your private space that requires organization, then do a thorough clean-up by following these simple steps:

1. Clear out or seal off the whole area that needs organizing. (You'll place anything you want to back in a bit, but it's good to have a blank slate to work with.)

2. Separate everything into three pile groups: one for the things you wish to retain, one for the things you can throw away, and one for the things you can give to a needy person.

3. Decide on an organizational structure. Use several-colored folders for various classes or arrange containers on bookshelves to keep related materials.

4. Choose a proper location for the objects you wish to preserve. For instance, all your video games should go in the same basket on the shelf, finished work files should go on one side of a folder, and incomplete work on the other.

5. Keep the products that fit your system and store them while removing the rest. Generally speaking, you need to eliminate anything you last utilized six months ago.

6. Check whether the space is still orderly a week later. If required, repeat steps 1-4.

7. Once you can effectively maintain this area's organization by investing very little time per week, use the same strategy in some other sites. Begin with the parts of your daily life that are most important.

Try this approach for at least a few weeks. If, after this period, you discover that it is ineffective for you, talk to your parents about finding an alternative method of organization. Make sure the technique you choose is simple to remember.

Added Tasks

Create a duplicate of the diagram below.

Keep records of the aspects of your life that require frequent organization using this chart and the organizing technique just discussed. Choose only one or two crucial topics to focus on for the first month (or write your own). Check the boxes for the week by placing a checkmark whenever you've finished organizing an area. As you become more adept at arranging your life, try adding a new site each month.

Area to be structured	**Week 1**	**Week 2**	**Week 3**	**Week 4**
Binder				
Desk				
Bedroom				
Desk				
Locker				
Backpack				

Write about your feelings after the organization, as mentioned above.

____

____

____

____

What adjustments may you make starting next month?

____

____

____

____

Activity 6: Organizing Resources

For your knowledge

Various tools are available in this technological era to aid in keeping individuals organized. Find out which are most appropriate for you by experimenting—finding a program that will enable you to keep a record, including all your obligations, in one convenient location.

Carlos, a child, had trouble keeping track of everything he needed to do and remember. One day he eventually decided to become more organized after being late for school again. That evening, he sat at the table with his father, and they explored several choices.

Carlos tried to use the planner his school had given him at the start of the school year for the next several weeks. It worked for some time, but he continued to appear to forget essential things because he forgot to check his planner for what he required or he forgot to record the events occurring.

Afterward, Carlos's parents bought him an electronic planner. They sat on the floor with him to demonstrate how to input all his engagements, school assignments, tasks, and responsibilities in the planner. Then, before all these chores were due, they created reminders that would sound at certain times. Carlos started entering his duties into the digital planner. Carlos liked the alarm feature since it gave a gentle reminder to check his organizer to see what needed to be done. He quickly improved his ability to recall homework and other responsibilities.

Your tasks

The list of instruments that individuals often utilize to assist them in organizing is provided below. Check the box next to any that you presently use.

A paper calendar

A printed calendar is an easy way to take a brief look at long-term planning.

An electronic calendar

The ability to set reminders on an electronic calendar is helpful.

A mobile phone

The calendar feature on a mobile phone will vibrate or beep to notify you of the events you've added.

Adhesive notes

Sticky and adhesive notes work well for writing reminders and sticking them on a planner or calendar.

A suitcase:

It can keep your work and school supplies for quick access.

An area for takeoff or landing:

Where you put everything, you require to leave home is a landing area or takeoff pad.

Hooks:

Keys, coats, and bags may all be hung on hooks to make them easier to find.

Desk organization:

Staplers, safety pins, and cutters are valuable tools in a desk organizer.

Baskets:

You can store small goods in baskets.

Bookcases:

Bookshelves are wonderful storage spaces for objects you wish to exhibit (such as trophies) and baskets filled with small things and books.

Office trays:

Desk or office trays are practical for storing documents you need to locate quickly.

File cabinets:

You may hide away important papers and records in a secure filing cabinet.

Task lists:

Making a list of your daily tasks can help you stay organized.

Over-the-door shoe storage:

For minor, quickly misplaced things you need to retrieve fast, an over-the-door shoe organizer works well (not just shoes).

A collapsible file:

An accordion or collapsible file is a portable organizing solution you can take in your bag.

Select one or two tools from the list mentioned above to supplement the ones you currently use.

How might they be used to keep you organized?

If you clarify that you're attempting to become more organized, your parent will probably be happy to assist you in getting these tools (if required). Try utilizing these tools regularly for a week and observe the results.

There is more to do.

Answer the following questions after experimenting with a few new tools from the last assignment.

Which of the following tools did you find to be most effective, and why?

Which didn't work out so well for you, and why do you think that is?

Keep experimenting with various tools unless you discover a few that best assist you in maintaining your organization. Before switching to a new device, be sure to practice using each one every day for at least a week to allow it time to function. Consider ways to utilize the things you already have in innovative ways. For instance, use a shoe organizer to arrange shoes and a study aid: Place a flash card and a piece of candy in each slot. Use the cards to quiz yourself; if you correctly respond to the questions, you get candy. Encouragement and organization in one convenient spot!

Activity 7: What Are Your Time Management Skills?

Just so you know

Understanding how to spend your time effectively is a sign of having good time management skills.

You can procrastinate by engaging in activities such as watching too much television, playing too many video games, or surfing the internet rather than completing tasks that will help you to achieve your objectives.

Beth, a fifteen-year-old, rose early, ate breakfast, and started preparing for school. She got a text message from her buddy Ashley as she was about to depart. Beth opted to reply to Ashley's SMS, which caused her to be delayed and miss the school bus. As a result of the fact that she had to wait for her mother to complete getting prepared for the job before she could catch a ride to school, Beth arrived at school late and was required to obtain a pass from the office.

Beth went by her buddy Tami's house on the way home from school to play a few video games. Beth's mother summoned her for supper at six, and she left to go home.

After eating dinner, Beth turned on the TV to see her show of choice. After that, she watched two more programs. At 10 o'clock, her mother finally inquired about the status of her homework.

She said, "Yes, I believe I did it."

Beth realized she had a history exam the next day as she was getting ready for bed. She now had to make a difficult choice: study late or go to bed. She decided she was too exhausted to learn and would try her guesses in the exam.

Beth's history exam result could have been better.

Beth has to work on her time management skills while she's not in class.

Your tasks

If you often indulge in the following activities, check the box next to them. Tasks that take up time but don't assist you in achieving your goals are referred to as "time wasters." The productive functions that can help you accomplish your goals are "time users."

Fill in the spaces with other tasks you engage in according to the category.

Time Wasters

- Watching TV
- Hobbies that include playing video games
- Texting friends and fellows
- Searching the web
- Spending excessive time on the phone

____

____

____

Time Users

- Finishing homework
- Performing music practice
- Preparation for an examination
- Organizing the home
- Doing a craft project

____

____

____

If the first column has more checks than the second, you're wasting too much time on activities that won't help you succeed at school and in your personal life.

Be aware that depending on how you utilize them, many activities, including those mentioned above, may either be "time users" or "time wasters." It would likely be deemed a "time waster" if you were utilizing the activity to put off doing a job that you needed to be doing, such as using housework as a justification to avoid making a dreaded but essential phone call. However, if something like watching TV or surfing the internet is necessary for work, it is most certainly categorized as a "time user."
There is much to do.

Putting tasks in order of importance involves deciding which ones are (1) most urgent and need your immediate attention and (2) least urgent but still require completion.
Please take a look at the schedule of Beth's day below. To help her prioritize:

Put a 1 next to high-priority tasks, a 2 next to medium-priority charges, and a 3 next to low-priority jobs.

Prioritize your list of the many tasks you must identically do every day.
Respond to the final questions.

Beth's Projects

__________ Prepare for the exam.

__________Check school uniform.

__________Take part in playing a video game.

__________Get up and have breakfast.

__________Stop by the office to obtain a pass.

__________Email your teacher.

__________Have dinner.

__________Board the bus.

__________Get to bed in time for sleep.

My Projects

What kind of tasks did you mark as grade 1?
Why did you believe these efforts to be of utmost importance?

What kind of tasks did you mark as grade 2?
Why did you provide a moderate importance rating for these actions?

Which tasks did you mark as grade 3?
Why did you consider these activities to be of low priority?
Describe a few of the factors that might elevate one activity above another.

Activity 8: Setting Aside Time

Just so you understand

Children with executive functioning often struggle to schedule. That includes how, when, and where to complete tasks. A timetable may be a handy tool because of these factors. Knowing what's coming up at a glance might be incredibly useful and make you feel less stressed.

When she was younger, Arianne's mother used to arrange her appointments, play dates, and sporting events. Her mother anticipated that now that she was thirteen, she would start completing these tasks alone. Her mother even bought her a large wall calendar so she could keep records of her schedule. Where would she begin? It needed to be clarified with Arianne. Arianne invited her friend Tina over to assist her in filling up her calendar since Tina was excellent at planning and managing her time. The first stage, according to Tina, was to list the tasks that needed to be completed on a particular day and time. After Arianne had finished them, Tina advised her to include all the duties she needed to achieve—not just those that were to be done by a particular day and time. Only after that could Arianne enter her to-do list, scheduling her activities around those previously scheduled. It would then prepare the whole plan for Arianne's month. Everything that arose at the last minute could be added once she made sure it fitted somewhere.

Your tasks

Here is Arianne's calendar, complete with the tasks she must do at specified times. Support Arianne in completing the remaining tasks on her schedule by adding the flexible jobs she must do and the activities she desires to accomplish, which are mentioned just after the calendar.

Monday	*Tuesday*	*Wednesday*	*Thursday*	*Friday*	*Saturday*	*Sunday*
	1	2 Snooker Practice 6 p.m. - 8 p.m.	3	4	5	6 Snooker Game 1 p.m. - 3 p.m.
7 Church 9 a.m.- 11 a.m.	8	9 Snooker Practice 6 p.m. - 8 p.m.	10	11 Mom's Birthday Dinner 9 p.m.- 11 p.m.	12	13 Snooker Game 1 p.m. - 3 p.m.
14 Church 9 a.m.- 11 a.m.	15 English Test	16 Snooker Practice 6 p.m. - 8 p.m.	17	18	19	20 Snooker Game 1 p.m. - 3 p.m.
21 Church	22	23	24	25	26	27

- Tidy up my bedroom (once a week)
- Walk my dog (Daily in the evening)
- View my favorite program (Wednesdays 7:00–8:00 p.m.)
- Review for the physics exam (Three nights weekly)
- Visit the cinema with Tina (open Saturday and Sunday)
- Get ready for the speech at her school (two nights a week from the seventh through the twenty-eight)

9 a.m.- 11 a.m.	Speech in English	Snooker Practice 6 p.m. - 8 p.m.		Science Test		Snooker Game 1 p.m. - 3 p.m.
28 Church 9 a.m.- 11 a.m.	29	30 Snooker Practice 6 p.m. - 8 p.m.				

Added tasks

It's your time now. Create a duplicate of the calendar layout below. Write down everything you are required to do, followed by everything you want to accomplish, after giving it a month and date label. It will serve as a visual prompt for completing specific tasks. You may buy a wall calendar or repeat this step for each month.

Sunday	*Monday*	*Tuesday*	*Wednesday*	*Thursday*	*Friday*	*Saturday*

Activity 9: Everyday Preparation

Just so you realize

Although a calendar is necessary for long-term scheduling, having a daily planner is also beneficial. Keeping a record of what you have to accomplish each day may be done using a daily planner. There are many distinct types of planners. A planner could be a physical journal, an electronic gadget, or a software application for your desktop, cellphone, or tablet. Use the one that suits you the best after you've found it.

Eighth-grader Raven had been concentrating on her executive functioning for several weeks. Her school counselor, Mrs. Thrasher, had given the weekly projects that helped her learn how to plan her present and future, establish long-term objectives, and consistently do her coursework and assignments. Mrs. Thrasher thought Raven was now prepared to begin organizing her work independently. She explained the importance of having a daily planner to Raven. Raven demonstrated how to record appointments, tasks, and assignments in a planner and mark them as completed. Mrs. Thrasher checked in on Raven each day for the next week as she practiced using a planner. On Friday, Raven received a gift from Mrs. Thrasher for accurately filling up her calendar throughout the week and doing all the chores she had listed.

After a few weeks of work, Raven mastered the art of daily planning and utilizing her calendar to keep on track.

Your tasks

Here is some practice using a fundamental planner structure. Specify up to 10 chores you must do between the time you wake up and the moment you go to bed tomorrow on the accompanying chart in the appropriate order. Include the duration for each while writing them. Tomorrow, after finishing a task tick the box next to it in the "Done" column.

Done	Task	Time
	Get Up	5 a.m.

Added tasks

Even if a planner is helpful, you still cannot complete a job if you don't possess the essential supplies. For instance, you must have your history notes or book to prepare for a history exam.

To ensure you have all the necessary supplies the next time, choose one of the jobs you outlined in the last exercise and respond to the questions below.

Assignment to be finished:

- In which time frame must this assignment be completed?
- What supplies do I require to complete this project?
- Where can I purchase these goods?
- Who might assist me in accomplishing this task?

Where do emotions originate?

For Your Knowledge

Feelings are a kind of emotional energy, and learning how to manage them properly is essential to maturity. Kids who struggle with executive functioning tasks have not yet mastered the capacity to control the intense emotions that may surface in certain circumstances. Understanding the source of your feelings is a fundamental first step in learning to regulate them.

Our minds function like computer algorithms. Computer outputs (what is seen on the screen, for instance) rely on the sort of program running and the input (what we type in, for example). The software contains guidelines for how to handle the information and input. Similarly, how we think about the events in our lives affects how we feel about them and behave. Negative sentiments and actions result when we "run" negative (irrational) ideas about the events in our life. Positive attitudes and actions result from running positive (logical) thoughts about the occurrences in our life.
Our minds often make sentences that include "should," "must," "ought to do," and other unquestionable imperatives. These laws often govern how other people behave toward us. Even though we might be accustomed to believing that everyone else should, might, or is supposed to act a particular way, the reality is that we do not influence others. Furthermore, we can alter our thought processes, impacting our emotions.

Let's take the scenario when a child calls you a bad name. It's unjust that he called you a bad name if your mind operates on an absolutes-based program. You could think, "He shouldn't call me that." You incite sentiments of rage against the child by saying this to yourself since he is disobeying the rule. Additionally, if you think what he stated is accurate, you can develop negative thoughts against yourself. If this keeps happening, you can inevitably decide to act negatively or inappropriately to address the circumstance. It develops into a vicious cycle that is difficult to end.

However, you may begin to alter your response to challenging circumstances with practice. Reminding yourself that you do not influence other people is the first step. The second step is refuting the other people's claims. Just because someone says something, it doesn't mean it is true. You can think, "I do not even enjoy getting called bad names, but I can't regulate other individuals, and what he stated is not true," instead of, "He shouldn't call me a bad name." By altering your ideas, you'll switch from the damaging emotions of wrath and self-hatred to the less harmful feeling of irritation.

Additionally, you'll be far less inclined to adopt bad habits, which will help to disrupt the cycle. Be cautious, and don't anticipate miracles.

These adjustments will be made, albeit gradually and after much practice.

Your Tasks

After reading each row of the accompanying chart, imagine what you would do or feel if the events were presented in the first column and you prescribed the thinking in the second column. Fill out the third column with your response.

Events	Irrational Behavior	Behavior or feeling
Someone makes insulting remarks about you.	His inability to do so.	
Your parents are shouting at you.	That is unjust.	
Your friendship with your pal ends.	I am not likable.	
Your milk is spilled	I'm such a moron.	
You score an F on your physics exam.	I ought to have had higher marks.	
Events	Rational Behavior	
Someone makes insulting remarks about you.	Oh my, he has a problem.	
Your parents are shouting at you.	I often irritate my parents.	
Your friendship with your pal ends.	I'm still a cute little kid.	
Your milk is spilt.	That is unfortunate.	
You score an F on your physics exam.	I'll have to do additional studying for the upcoming physics exam.	

For instance, the first one has already been completed for you.

Added tasks

Consider any emotion you can recall experiencing throughout the previous week. Outline, and then for everyone, explain the circumstances that, in your opinion, led to that emotion.

Sensational Situation

1.

2.

3.

4.

5.

List the ideas you can recall experiencing in every one of the following scenarios:

1.

2.

3.

4.

5.

Find the absolute feelings in your ideas (the "musts" or "shoulds"). Name them.

Pick one of your ideas, including an absolute, and then recast it in kinder, more tolerant language.

Is there a variation in how you think about it now?

____

____

____

____

Try rephrasing the following points in kinder, more understanding ways, and see how your reactions could change the next time you find yourself in similar circumstances.

____

____

____

____

Activity 10: Recognizing Your Emotions

For Your Knowledge

Emotional strength is represented through feelings. Depending on your emotions, they indicate that something within your life must either continue or change. Although sentiments aren't good or evil, your actions with them may have positive or adverse effects.It helps you fully comprehend your emotions to control them.

Seventh-grade Jacob had just left Mr. Bright's language art course late because the remaining students refused to comply with his request for them to be silent.

As a result, Mr. Bright forced the whole class to wait until after the bell. Scott, a fellow seventh-grader, ran straight into Jacob while hurrying to reach Mrs. Delaney's math class on time. Scott's collision caused Jacob's textbooks and notes to scatter throughout the floor. Scott did not even acknowledge that he had run into Jacob and didn't even attempt to apologize. Jacob began yelling at Scott as he proceeded on his journey.

Stop, you fool! And collect my books.

Scott ignored it and carried on going. Jacob could no longer strike the bell when he collected all his books and papers. He reached two minutes late for Mrs. Delaney's class.

Mrs. Delaney said to him as he entered, "Jacob, please give me your behavior card."

However, Mrs. D., somebody threw my textbooks on the ground, which is why I'm running late.

No debates, Jacob. Please provide hand over your behavior card.

Mrs. Delaney received the card that Jacob had dug out and scribbled one of the little Xs in the corner.

By this point, Jacob became so furious over what had occurred that he could not concentrate on arithmetic.

Afterward, as he made his way to lunch, he resented Mrs. Delaney for writing on his card about an incident that wasn't even his fault. He looked at Scott, joking and laughing with a buddy as he approached the lunch line. Jacob came to Scott directly and gave him a mighty shove.

When Scott turned back, he said, "Jerk, what was that for?"

"For being stupid," Jacob spat.

Both boys started shoving each other soon after. Mr. Bright entered and led the group to the office where the principal was waiting.

Your Tasks

Mark all the terms that best capture Jacob's feelings throughout the preceding narrative.

Cheerful
Depressed
Annoyed
Dissatisfied
Irritated
Terrified
Anxious
Enthusiastic
Humiliated
Aggravated
Uncertain

Nervous

Mediocre

Pleased

Prohibited

In what portion did you mark those you wanted to remember?

____

____

____

____

Do you believe that many emotions may exist simultaneously? Why, or why not?

____

____

____

____

What narrative event(s) do you think "caused" Jacob to retaliate in the manner he did?

____

____

____

____

What did Jacob say to himself before, throughout, and after every instance in the narrative?

____

____

____

____

For each instance in the tale, list one or two things Jacob could have done better.

Added tasks

Use colored markers and pencils to list all the recent emotions you've felt in the below-mentioned space. Write the message you believe each emotion is attempting to convey to you right next to it. If you typed FRUSTRATION, the message may be that you should seek assistance with anything that is bothering you.

If you write HAPPY, it might mean that something in your life is going well. Then underline any messages that suggest a necessary change in your life. Consider how you can modify what needs to be changed in your life. Ask for assistance if you are unable to alter them on your own.

....

....

....

....

……………………………………………………………………
…………………………………
……………………………………………………………………
…………………………………
……………………………………………………………………
…………………………………
……………………………………………………………………
…………………………………
……………………………………………………………………
………………………………...
……………………………………………………………………
…………………………………

Activity 11: Controlling your negative emotions

For Your Knowledge

There will always be moments when it's almost difficult to stop your bad sentiments, no matter how much you try or how often you practice doing so. They could appear when your instructor reminds you for the hundredth time that you must try a little harder to turn in your assignments on time or when your parents chastise you for not doing your responsibilities. Remember that we all sometimes experience unpleasant emotions. Therefore, learning how to handle them is a valuable skill to have.

According to studies, players who picture winning a significant game before playing it are more likely to succeed since they have already viewed a positive result. We may conjure up the outcomes we want to see with mental visualization. It applies to almost every circumstance. Before starting the assignment, picture yourself finishing it effectively if you wish for more excellent scores. Even though you are still required to put in the same amount of work, you might find that you have a more incredible drive to succeed. Additionally, visualization may assist you in developing good sentiments about yourself and your circumstance.

Your Tasks

Draw a circle around every unfavorable emotion you've had in the last two weeks.

Embarrassed

Insulted

Ashamed

Disrespected

Laid down

Harassed

Undervalued

Strained out

Overstretched

Unaccompanied

Muddled

Disheartened

Disregarded

Forbidden

Abhorrent

Censured

Refereed

Frightened

Terrified

Susceptible

Untrusted

Write about the circumstances that led to the emotions you circled.

____

____

____

____

What might you have done differently in that circumstance to have had a better result?

____

____

____

____

Rewrite your story as if you would react differently and see if it sounds any better.

____

____

____

____

Please read through the scenario, as it has been rewritten multiple times. Then, close your eyes and visualize this scenario. Imagine performing what you stated. You might have done something different in the plan as clearly and in detail as you can.

You should note any changes in your emotions between the actual scenario and the envisioned one in writing. What do you suppose the causes of these variations are?

____

____

____

____

More to do

Our bodies stiffen up when we feel unfavorable emotions.

Try the subsequent progressive relaxation practice to relieve body tension brought on by unpleasant feelings. It can work best if you perform it while listening to calming music.

Take a seat or lie down in a relaxed posture. Loosen up any garments that are too snug. Close your eyes. Attempt to relax and allow all of your worries and concerns to go.

2. Inhale deeply; hold your breath for a moment, and then exhale. Repeat twice. Imagine your body becoming more relaxed with each inhalation.

3. Contract your lower legs. Your feet, fingertips, ankles, and calves should all be tightened as much as possible. Imagine trying to drag your toes apart

and strain every tissue in your lower thighs. Keep this tension in your body as you inhale deeply and hold that breath for a few seconds. As you exhale, let go of any stress you may be having in your lower thighs. Keep Repeating.

4. Pull your buttocks and thighs to build a strain. Maintain this strain whenever you draw in a sharp intake of breath and maintain it for the duration of one beat. As you exhale, let go of any tension you may be holding in your thighs and buttocks. Keep Repeating.

5.Tighten your shoulders and your abdominal muscles. Maintain this strain as you draw a deep breath and hold it for the beat. As you exhale, let go of all the tension that has built up in your chest and belly. Repeat.

6. Contract every muscle in your arms, wrists, shoulders, and fingers, starting at your shoulders and working your way down while forming a fist with both hands. Maintain this tension as you draw a deep breath and hold it for the beat. As you exhale, let go of all the stress that has built up in your arms, wrists, shoulders and, fingers. Keep repeating.

7. Stress your facial muscles and those in your neck and head. Maintain this strain as you draw a deep breath and hold it for the beat. As you exhale, let go of all the stress that has built up in your head, neck, and face. Repeat.

8. Quietly check your physique for any strain that may be left. Focus on releasing any tension you detect from your body. Inhale deeply three more times, then exhale. When you stand up, you'll feel at ease. You'll

experience happiness and less tension. You can feel thoroughly and worry-free while you drift off to sleep or go on with your day.

Try this relaxing technique whenever you feel a nasty mood coming on. If you can't do that right away after experiencing a bad feeling, do it every night before going to bed. You should start to feel less troubled by unpleasant feelings after some time.

Activity 12: Describe An Impulse

For Your Knowledge

A sudden want to move one's body or take some action is referred to as an impulse. Impulsive people act on their thoughts without considering the future repercussions. If you're impulsive, you usually take action before assessing whether it is the right course. Children who behave rashly often find themselves in hot water with their parents, instructors, or the authorities.

Chiara, a seventh-grade student, has a habit of disrupting adults. She reasoned that she could forget what was on her mind if she didn't express it. Chiara also spoke incoherently in class. Chiara would know the answer even before the instructor could complete her question. Similarly to this, she often began tasks before reading all of the instructions. Consequently, she sometimes failed to complete the work as instructed, negatively impacting her marks.

Chiara often had a conflict with her mom, dad, and professors due to poor choices that she might have avoided. She would, for instance, sneak away from home after school to visit a friend's house or copy other kids' work in class. Chiara once grabbed a ring from a shop without paying for it. Although they didn't desire to get into trouble with her when she behaved impulsively, her friends found it difficult to be around her.

Your task

Suppose that the following shape represents your body. Mark the body parts where you are compelled to move or take action.

List the impulsive actions you took today (that are done without thinking of the consequences).

1.
2.
3.
4.
5.

There is much to do

Teens who behave impulsively are often encouraged to stop, but it's not always easy.

It requires time to break a bad habit. Nevertheless, keeping STOP in mind might enable you to choose wisely more often. Stop, Think, Observe, and plan is known as STOP.

S—Stop whatever you're doing, please.
T—Think about the reasons for your recent actions.
O—Observe how the individuals involved were impacted by what you have just done.

P— Plan what you'll be doing the following time differently.

Test it now

Consider that you have just carried out one of the impulsive behaviors you listed in the last exercise. Respond to the following questions in the STOP style to assist you in coming up with a more effective course of action. One that will help you achieves your goals without suffering the repercussions or achieving them later.

Stop all the things you're doing.

What was the impulsive act that you just did?

Think about the motivations behind your most recent action.

Why did you do something like that? (Check the boxes next to each item that applies.)

Escaping a situation
Avoiding a peer
Avoiding a task
Piquing an adult's interest
Attracting the attention of others
Obtaining things/doing things.
Motivating yourself about something

Observe the effects of what you just performed on the concerned parties.

What effects do your impulsive tasks have on those involved?

Plan what you can change for the future.

If you do not, however, succeed right away. Please describe what you'll do in its place to achieve your goals in the future.

Activity 13: What to do if you fail the first time

For Your Understanding

There may be moments when everything goes according to plan, and sometimes you must catch up on your objectives. When it occurs, you should gather your strength and make another attempt. It's unnecessary to fully surrender to your failure because you weren't successful the first time. There is always a possibility of getting back on track.

Wendy, a fourteen-year-old, devoted much effort to honing her executive abilities. She worked on arranging her resources and scheduling her daily tasks. Wendy worked on strengthening her memories. She even began establishing objectives for herself. But no matter how hard Wendy tried, Wendy could not succeed in several of her relatively small purposes.

She had, for instance, vowed to work out six days a week for an entire year, but after merely one month, she began coming up with justifications: She first persuaded herself that she was overwhelmed with schoolwork to do and lacked time to exercise.

She reasoned, "I'm not obtaining any results; why even bother?"

Wendy's father called her one day to discuss this after seeing that she wasn't achieving the objectives she had set for herself. He stated that she seemed to be undermining her effort to exercise by explaining why she could not exercise. Wendy and her father discussed Wendy's objective. Having all of her other responsibilities, Wendy's aim of exercising six days per week turned out to be lofty. Wendy changed her objective from exercising six days per week to 3 days per week. She also permitted herself to skip an exercise if anything came up.

Despite her numerous responsibilities, Wendy worked out two or three days weekly. She saw that when her workout objective was more attainable, she was more motivated to work out and seemed to be growing fitter, and other aspects of her life were coming together excellently.

Your tasks

Why do you believe you failed at particular activities? Explain in writing.

____

____

____

____

If you were to repeat those activities, list the names of the persons in your life who might aid you.

List one action you want to do yet again with the assistance of some or all

of these folks.

Describe the changes you'll make this time.

Write the meaning of "sabotage" below after looking it up in the dictionary.

What actions do you believe you may have taken to sabotage the events that didn't go as you had intended?

____

____

____

____

Talk to a trustworthy adult about what you have done differently to make those activities go more smoothly or what you could attempt next time. Put their suggestions in the space below.

____

____

____

____

Jot down any instances in which you may have degraded or "beaten" yourself up for doing poorly on any exercises.

____

____

____

____

You'll be able to do more because you'll feel better about yourself and what you do if you are kinder and more supportive of yourself. How might you treat yourself with more extraordinary kindness and motivate yourself to engage in those hobbies again?

Activity 14: Oppress IT!

Just so you understand

Consider yourself as the captain of a ship representing your life. Not really that long ago, you used to sail this ship aimlessly, going wherever the wind led you because you needed to figure out where you intended to take it. You've chosen a few locations now (your goals). But consider a scenario where a water ship such as this one lacks an electronics tracking system. How would you go to your destination then? You're the commander, after all! You must chart your route. You must continue to guide the voyage in the proper orientation unless you arrive at your destination if you want to remain on course, even when the water is choppy, and the climate is ominous. You can only succeed if you create objectives and follow through on them.

You should use several additional executive skills to understand how to plan and accomplish objectives. It would be best if you had the mental capabilities to think about what you intend and who you are, organize your thoughts, regulate your time, and start and continue actions that get you closer to your goal.

Your ability to remember this skill will increase as you learn and use the mnemonic STICK. Specific details, Timetable, I Could Do It, Computable, and know Your Limitations are the acronyms for STICK.

S—Specifics: It would be best if you had a clear goal in your mind before you can create a plan. It is insufficient to declare, "Maybe someday I'll take action about this." You must be exceptionally clear about what you desire. Does your objective, for instance, entail specific people, locations, or things? What specific steps will you take to accomplish it?

T – Time axis: Goals must have a deadline; else, they are merely grand aspirations. While it's fun to speculate about your life in the coming years, if you don't set a deadline for when you want to accomplish certain things, those fantasies will remain dreams.

I—I Could Do It: I am confident in my ability to do the task. Setting unachievable objectives puts you in a riskier position than not setting any targets. For instance, since it is illegal for anybody under sixteen to receive a license, it is not a good idea to establish a goal of learning to drive before age sixteen.

C—Calculable: If an objective is written to make it possible to assess your development realistically, it is calculable. If your objective is ambiguous or intangible, such as "To do better at school," Consider the indicators that demonstrate you are progressing towards or have achieved your objective. It is possible to measure progress towards a goal such as "to obtain Bs in at least three of my courses this semester."

K—Know your boundaries: You would only set yourself up for failure if you select a goal that would be incredibly difficult for you to accomplish. For many individuals, it is not feasible to achieve the objective of being able to leap high enough to touch the ceiling. On the other hand, a goal that does not involve a significant amount of work from you or does not test your capabilities is not particularly relevant to your personal development. There ought to be a middle ground.

Your tasks

According to studies, setting and tracking objectives increases a person's likelihood of success. By writing down your goals, you may offer yourself the most significant opportunity of making your dreams come true.

For a couple of minutes, close your eyes and see the future you described in the preceding exercise. Imagine your surroundings and activities using all of your sensations. Open up your eyes, and then make a list of what you observed.

Now that you have this knowledge, establish a STICK objective for yourself. Describe as much information as possible about a particular action you may see yourself performing.

S—Specifics

Your aim should begin with the phrase "I will." Avoid using negative words like "not" while stating your purpose; instead, use optimistic language.

I will.....

T–Time axis

When do you anticipate finishing this?

I would like to complete this by...

Are you truly capable of doing this? (Circle the response)

No

Yes

Might be

Continue to the following stage if the answer is yes. If you answered "no," could you please explain why? What would need to be altered about your objective from no to become yes? If you need help to accomplish your purpose, go back and change your time frame or specifications.

____

____

____

____

C—Calculable

How would you recognize this since you've accomplished this objective?

K— Know your limitations.

Consider yourself Goldilocks: not too challenging or straightforward, but just about perfect. Is reaching this objective a little struggle for you but not too much of a battle? (Circle the response.)

No

Yes

Might be

If the answer is affirmative, you have achieved your STICK aim. If you replied "no," could you please explain why? What would need to be altered about your objective for a nope or perhaps to become a yes? Revise your

Timetable or parameters once again until your aim is challenging but realistic

Added tasks

There isn't a clear line between "long-term" and "short-term." The short-term goals that are most likely to be achieved are those that can be completed in less than a year. It indicates that the objective you listed in the last application is a long-term objective. Write a short-term goal now by using the same process. It may be as simple as setting aside enough money to buy a friend or loved one a reasonably priced gift.

Short-term objective

S—Specifics

What precisely are you going to do?

I will

T—Time frame

When do you anticipate having it completed? The ideal would be somewhere under a year.

I would like to complete it by….

Is this objective feasible? (Underline the response.)

True

False

Maybe

Continue to the following stage if the answer is yes. If your answer is no, please explain why. What would need to be altered about your objective for a no or a maybe to become a yes? If you need help to accomplish your goal, go back and change your time frame or specifications.

____

____

____

____

C—Calculable

When you have reached your objective, how will you recognize that you have done so?

K—Know your limitations.

Does achieving this objective require you to stretch, but not too far? (Circle the response.)

No

Yes

Might be

Congrats! You've achieved your relatively brief STICK objective if the answer is yes. If your answer is no, please explain why. What would need to be altered about your aim for a nope or a probable to become a yes? Revise your Timetable or parameters once again till your objective is challenging but realistic.

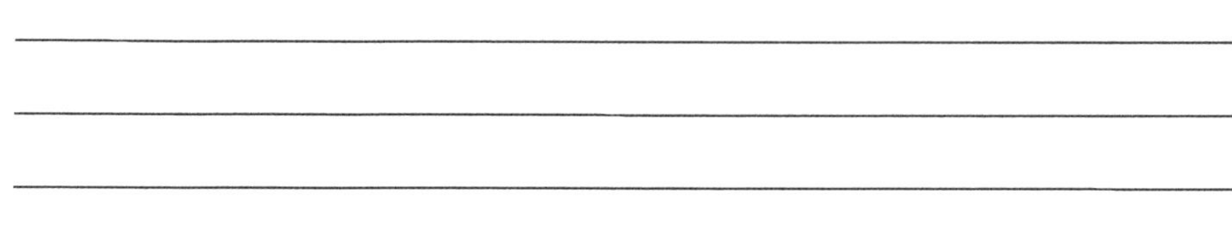

Activity 15: Letter to yourself

Just so you understand

You can sometimes believe that things will always be the same. But developing and accomplishing objectives requires taking a step back and considering how things could change. Imagine or dream about the future by posing the question, "What if...?". It may spark concepts that result in objectives.

Nick, fourteen years old, was quite frustrated. He had made several attempts to modify his life, but he had never been able to keep it up. In a desperate effort, he begged his elder brother David for assistance.

David asked Nick to write down all he wished he could alter about his lifestyle as they sat together. They then brainstormed ideas for possible actions Nick could take to bring about those improvements. His brother provided a list of potential allies for Nick. Last but not least, they created a checklist Nick might use to keep himself on course.

Nick eventually began acting in a manner that enabled him to obtain the things he desired, and he began to feel much superior concerning himself and his destiny.

For you to do

Compose a letter to yourself that you can use in the future. The statement describes your career goals for the next seven to eight years. Attempt to integrate all facets of your life (family, work, school, relationships, hobbies, and many more).

Dear, ___________

I envision the following for you in the future:

Sincerely,

____

More to do

Your letter included what may be referred to as your futuristic dreams. Your aspirations for the long term are everything you hope for. One thing that distinguishes a dream from a goal is that it does not have a specific plan. A vision becomes a goal once you give it a strategy and decide what actions you must take to make it come true. Sometimes it takes work to turn a plan into reality.

Describe the visions you mentioned in the letter.

___

___

___

What actions will you be required to take to make these aspirations come true?

___

___

___

___

Give the names of the persons in your personal life who can lend a hand.

___

___

___

___

What further tasks or projects must you do to complete these steps?

____

____

____

____

Activity 16: Learn new skills for an old brain

Just so you understand

Learning how your brain absorbs new information might help you succeed in various endeavors.

Some children's brains function best when exposed to visual or auditory information. Some brains are more suited to active learning. You may save a lot of time and effort by using several "tricks" to teach your brain to recall information quickly.

Most of the time, Laura, a thirteen-year-old girl, found it difficult to recall what she required and what she had to do next. She was remiss in doing at least one of her duties daily. Laura finally gave up because of how much she had forgotten. She chose to schedule a meeting with her school counselor. Her counselor gave Laura tips on sharpening her memory throughout many appointments. Laura improved her memory dramatically over time. Even her mother remarked on how much she had improved. Her marks went up when Laura remembered to finish and submit her tasks.

Your tasks

People acknowledge it easier when the information is delivered in a manner that suits their learning style. Visual learners absorb information through their eyes and typically recall what they see. Auditory learners are those who take in information through their ears and prefer to memorize what they listen to, and tactile learners are those who abide in knowledge through their hands and tend to remember what they do.

Six memorization tips are provided here, two for each remembering style. Mark the three that you intend to attempt with a checkmark.

Visual aids for memory

Create a custom:

Put something there that you wouldn't normally expect to see, particularly something you have difficulty recalling to bring with you when you leave the house. For instance, if you often forget to take your finished schoolwork to school and leave it on your desk, place something you wouldn't typically see, such as a teddy bear, on your writing table as a reminder. You'll be able to recall your assignment whenever you see that teddy bear.

Apply color:

Anything you need to memorize should be color-coded. For instance, color all your appointments green and your obligations yellow on your planner. It will make it more straightforward to recall items and recognize them.

Audio memory techniques

Make a tune:

Create a song about something you want to memorize. For instance, alter a popular song's lyrics to help you remember a grocery list.

Send out reminders orally:

To hear and memorize, speak out loudly. Say something to yourself like, "I'm putting my shoes in the wardrobe," for instance, while placing your shoes back in the wardrobe.

Tactile memory techniques

Making it a routine:

Everything should have a habitation and you should keep each item there. For instance, if you bring your smartphone to school, always place it on the same table when you get back home, and if you take it out to use it, return it after you're done.

Engage your body:

Utilize various body parts to aid memory; start at your toes and work your way up. For instance, consider stamping on a chicken's fingers if you remember to purchase both stamps and chicken fingers. Being silly is a beautiful thing!

Added tasks

Try each memory technique you chose in the last exercise for the next several days or the next few items you need to remember, and then respond to the questions below.

Whichever trick or tricks did you find to be the most successful?

___

___

___

___

In what facets of your life have you found these memorizing methods to be most helpful?

___

___

___

___

Add anyone else's memory tips in addition to those you've previously attempted in the following area. Try to include the aspects of those techniques that worked best for you, whether Visual, aural, or tactile.

___

___

___

___

Activity 17 Utilizing Acronyms

Just so you understand

The word "mnemonic" derives from the Greek word "mnemonikos," which may be translated as "of or linked to memory." The English word "mnemonic" is pronounced, "nee-MON-ik." A mnemonic would be any suggestion or strategy that you use to assist in memorizing lists or other informative bits. You can also use Mnemonics to help you learn new material. Mnemonic devices are highly beneficial when remembering a supermarket's shopping list, a sequence of occasions (perhaps for an exam of history), a categorization of procedures, or something else. Mnemonic devices can help you recall a shopping list, a chronology of events, or processes. The use of mnemonic devices is often referred to as mnemonics, another word for practice.

The Honorable "Biv Roy G," you apologize and say, "Please excuse my darling Aunt Sally." Noodles have just been brought over to us by my ecstatic mother. Do you recognize any of the following proverbs? You may have acquired the knowledge necessary to employ these mnemonic strategies to assist you in recalling certain pieces of information. As a result of their catchy nature, they are easy to remember and quick to bring to your mind at the proper time.

There is a wide range of formats and dimensions available for mnemonic devices. The phrase "Biv Roy G" is an acronym, and every letter of that phrase represents a different term. It helps us remember the rainbow colors: blue, indigo, violet, red, orange, yellow, and green.

Acrostics are statements in which the first character of every letter stands for a particular word. For example, "Please excuse my darling Aunt Sally" and "My extremely pleased mommy just supported us noodles" are both acrostics. The following sequence should be used in mathematical operations: parenthesis, exponents, multiplication, division, addition, and subtraction. By stating something like, "My very pleased mommy just supported us noodles," we may be able to bring to mind the planets Mercury, Venus, Pluto, Mars, Jupiter, Saturn, Uranus, and Neptune. An illustration of a rhyming mnemonic that you may use to help recall a spelling guideline is "I before E unless after C or pronounced as A," which can be found in the words "neighbor" and "weigh." An illustration of a musical mnemonic would be the ABC song that you learned to assist you in remembering the alphabet's letters. Mnemonics help increase working memory since they allow you to keep information for extended periods, which is one of the main benefits of using them.

Tasks for you

Create mnemonics such as acrostics, lyrics, acronyms, or melodies to assist you in remembering the information in the below-mentioned lists. Suppose you connect your memorization strategy in some way to the material being studied. In that case, it will likely be easier for you to recall the information when it comes up in conversation. You might, for example, use the titles of former presidents in a song that pertains to the White House.

Ten states of USA (United States of America)

Arkansas, Arizona, Alaska, California, Idaho, Indiana, Iowa, Maryland, Mississippi, and Montana.

The Various Regions

America, Europe, Asia, Australia, Antarctica, North and South America, and Africa.

There are 15 Items That You Should purchase at the supermarket.

Food items include doughnuts, dish soap, milk, eggs, hamburger, bananas, ketchup, soda, shampoo, butter, buns, and paper plates.

Additional responsibilities

Researchers have shown that music and memory are connected significantly to each other. In most cases, you need to hear just a few notes of a piece of music you are already familiar with to recognize it immediately. In addition, if you are familiar with the song, you can remember all the words or most of them. Marketers employ jingles to capitalize on this connection and embed messages in customers' brains.

Select a task that you have to keep in mind to complete. It might be a responsibility, an assignment, or something significant. To help you remember that work better, compose a catchy song or jingle utilizing some of the terms and ideas linked with it. Utilize whatever musical style is acceptable (from rapping to country), but make sure the song is concise and exciting.

Jingle

Copy:...

....

....

....

Jingle

Style:..

....

....

....

.....

Activity 18: The focus of interest

For Your Knowledge

Children who struggle with executive functioning may have trouble concentrating and paying close attention. Additionally, they may appear unable to turn down environmental distractions (like the TV when it becomes time to complete schoolwork) or resist their want for stimulation. It's a good idea to exercise your ability to quiet your thoughts and concentrate your focus.

Henry, who was in seventh grade, was hyperactive and restless. When he had an idea, he would act on it right away. Henry would be in the vehicle and prepared to go in less than a minute if someone proposed going somewhere.

Henry was likewise unable to block off distractions. If he was in a room and saw motion in the corridor, he would check to find out what was happening. He would dash into the next room as soon as he heard the Television being turned on so he could see what was being shown.

Henry found it very difficult to accomplish anything. His instructors reported that he only partially or never completed his homework. Even though he was easily distracted by outside sounds or the Television, his parents struggled to persuade him to do his responsibilities. If Henry was incapable of paying attention, how did he ever complete tasks?

For you

To do this exercise, you'll need to locate an uninterrupted spot and some time to relax for around ten to fifteen minutes. A timer/stopwatch is also necessary.

Put a timer for fifteen minutes on a stopwatch. Sit silently (perhaps in a cozy chair) and permit your thoughts to meander while you take in your environment. Don't attempt to redirect or concentrate on any one subject when your attention is wandering; just be aware of it. Allow your focus to go where it wants to, and then let it return when this is ready. After fifteen minutes, make a list of everything that drew your interest.

Did anything appear to capture your concentration for a more extended period than others? So then, what kind of things are they?

____

____

____

____

Why do you believe those items captured your interest for a more extended period than others?

____

____

____

____

Added tasks

Although it takes time and effort, you can train your concentration. It requires practice, just like learning to do anything.

Maintain your seated position just as in the last exercise. Put on a fifteen-minute timer. After you have focused on something during this time, please make an effort to maintain it as long as possible.

Whether this is something you see, something you hear, or both, mentally take note of as many specifics of the subject of your attention as you can. Make an effort to list at least five different traits.

After you have investigated all aspects of whatever you are concentrating on, allow your attention to stray to the next object you see in your surroundings. Repeat the procedure once your fifteen minutes have passed. Explain the following two questions while doing this exercise for the first time

1. This time, how many items drew your attention? Mention them.

2. Did this include lesser or more items than the last activity? (Circle the response.)

More, **Less**

Attempt to do this activity each day for a week; when you've already done it a few times, check if you can concentrate on just one object in your surroundings for fifteen minutes. Then, respond to the questions that follow.

For the whole fifteen minutes, could you concentrate on just one thing? (Circle the response.)

No **Yes**

How did you focus on one thing while simultaneously blocking out everything else?

Practice concentration for fifteen minutes a day for a week, then twenty minutes a day for a week, then twenty-five minutes a day for a week. You will significantly improve your ability to focus on practically any task (or extend if you choose).

Activity 19: Working memory enhancement

For Your Knowledge

Information you intend to utilize or deal with quickly is kept in your working memory. For instance, working memory is used when you seek a phone number and remember it or say it to yourself before dialing it. While some individuals are inherently stronger at this, it can strengthen anybody's working memory with effort. A helpful talent to have is the ability to remember lists and other information when necessary.

Though Kristen performed exceptionally well in primary school, she began to have trouble with schoolwork. She would often fail to bring her homework. Even if she gets work from home, she would likely forget to complete it or submit it.

Kristen also needed help to follow instructions with much more than two stages. For instance, if her father instructed her to clean her room and wash the dishes after doing her schoolwork, she would accomplish her homework but neglect to complete the other tasks. Kristen became quite unhappy when the school notified her one day that she could not participate in the field trip; because she still needed to bring her signed permission slip for the class field trip.

Examination by the school counselor identified Kristen's working memory as a shortcoming. Kristen improved significantly at remembering her obligations after she started regularly performing cognitive tests.

Your Tasks

The list of words is on the next page. Try to remember the list after giving it a minute of study. Afterward, return to this page and list every phrase you can recall. The first time you do this exercise, it may go poorly, but if you do it once a week for a few weeks, you could discover that you grow much faster at memorizing lists.

Studying and repeating this list may aid your memory of the words on it, and understanding that our mind works best when given imagery may be of even greater use. Making a bizarre mental association with the things on the list is one strategy for remembering a list. For instance, if you need to recall getting your mom a head of lettuce, try seeing her with lettuce in place of her head. It also ties to another concept: remembering a list of objects by using certain body parts. It's easy to remember what you need to get at the grocery store if you imagine putting butter on your knees and milk on your feet.

Words List

Kitten

Utah

Carroty

Doggy

Bangladesh

Bananas

Reddish

Pink

Sledgehammer

Swindler

Twist

Donkey

Pears

Hitch

Glutton

Chimpanzee

Saying

Avocado

London

Grapefruit

Prestigious

Murky

Screwdrivers

Bloodshot

Microorganism

Bananas

Downhearted

Added task

The process of reducing massive amounts of data to more manageable chunks is called chunking. For example, if you divide a group of nine items into three groups of three, one group of four, and one group of five, it will be much simpler to remember the order in which they were presented afterward. When it comes to chunking anything, there is no one way superior to another; instead, you may chunk in any way you see fit. You will, however, have a better chance of remembering the knowledge. If you can digest it in manageable portions (chunks), you may find it easier to absorb. Try associating the characters of your nickname with the products you need to purchase at the supermarket.

When moving on to the next task, employ the same approach you succeeded with in the prior one. However, the information has been broken into manageable chunks for your benefit. Then, compare the results of this activity with the previous one to determine whether or not chunking helped you remember a massive amount of data.

Words List

Birds and Animals

Buffalo

Horse

Sea snake

Sparrow

Lizards

States of America

Arizona

Colorado

Arkansas

Connecticut

California

Delaware

Apparatuses

Sockets

Bradawl

Borer

Measuring Tape

Vices

Fruits

Oranges

Apples

Grapes

Mangoes

Water Melon

Colors

Green

Pink

Purple

Red

Indigo

Random Words

Babies

Sports Car

Shower

Today

Scissors

Likewise, the more frequently you chunk, the greater your level of expertise will get. Investigate several chunking strategies to find the one that works best for you. You might arrange items alphabetically or classify them according to other categories.

Activity 20: Prolonged Gratification

For your information

Acquiring what you desire gives you satisfaction. Kids who struggle with concentration often choose what they want to do above what they are required to accomplish simply because it's more enjoyable, intriguing, or rewarding. It's termed "immediate gratification" when you receive what you want right away, and it's the polar opposite of "delayed gratification (getting what you wish with delays)," which means waiting for what you desire.

Several psychologists conducted a study with a group of children long ago. During the experiment, researchers informed separate groups of kids that they would each get a marshmallow from an experimenter, who would then leave the room. They explained to the kids that they would reward them with an additional marshmallow if they could refrain from eating it until the researcher returned to the room. If they could not wait, they would get just one marshmallow. The marshmallow was consumed by several of the children before the investigator returned. On the other hand, some children were capable of waiting. The researchers who followed up with the kids years later discovered that those who stayed for the additional marshmallow performed better academically and had more career success.

What you need to do

Consider the activities you frequently engage in, despite the reality that you are well aware that you should not do (things like eating the marshmallow in the experiment described above).

Let's refer to these pursuits as "desired" activities. "Required" actions will be what we refer to as "things that you should be doing instead," and they include things like waiting for the experimenter to return.

Create a list of activities you "want" and things you "need" to do.

Want Actions		**Need Actions**
TV watching	Do Instead	**Dishwashing**
....	Do Instead	....
....	Do Instead	....
....	Do Instead	....
....	Do Instead	....

Additional tasks required

It might be challenging to master managing your "want" and "need" activities independently. Using a "want" activity as a reward for completing a "need" activity is one of the most effective strategies to get a "needed" task completed. You will get more of what you desire if you can learn to put off finishing "want" activities to accomplish "need" ones, much as the children in the marshmallows research.

You may set up prizes for completing the actions you need to accomplish by using the chart provided below.

If I proceed with this first	**I'll be able to accomplish this…**
Dishwashing	Play my favorite video game.

Activity 21: What surroundings do you have?

Just so you understand

You are in a digital age. You could come across TVs, laptops, cell phones, and other electronic equipment. Kids who already struggle with attention span issues may become much worse with these gadgets, which constantly bombard us with information from many sources.

Jamal, a seventh-grader, texted his buddies for several hours every day. He wrote about his professors, classes, tv watching, and meals; Jamal wrote to his professors about his homework and to his parents about his plans for the evening. He texted about almost anything.

Jamal also utilized a tablet for a variety of tasks. On this, he watched documentaries, texted his buddies, and played games.

Last but not least, Jamal frequently did his schoolwork while watching TV. He would hear his mother's voice asking him to turn off the TV to concentrate on his work, but he disregarded her.

Kids nowadays are used to and proficient with technology that many older people have difficulty mastering. However, many kids are unaware that attempting to concentrate on too many things at once might make it difficult for them to do so. It can improve your capacity to do the tasks you need to complete by practicing to "single project." Technology is terrific, but it has to be controlled and utilized sparingly.

For you

To what extent do you have access to the following technological devices? Indicate with a check mark. Add any equipment you own that still needs to be added to the list. Then, for a week, record how much time you spend using each of these gadgets daily.

kinds of equipment	Having access to or ownership of	Sat	Sun	Mon	Tues	Wed	Thu	Fri
Smartphone								
Personal Computer								
Laptop								
Tablet PC (Apple, Samsung, Sony)								
Ipad								
TV								
CD/DVD Player								
Transistor								
Video Games								

Is there somebody in your life who could be worried about how much time you spend using technology? If it is, then who exactly?

How can using these technology tools make it harder for you to focus on crucial tasks? (For instance, do you message your buddies when you must be completing your schoolwork or performing chores?). Include any suggestions for reducing your usage of these gadgets.

There is much more to do

Spend many hours (or possibly the whole day) without using technology. Then respond to the subsequent questions.

How difficult was it for you to spend quality time without using technology on a scale from zero to ten (where ten is very difficult)? (Underline the response)

0 1 2 3 4 5 6 7 8 9 10

What contributed to its difficulty or ease?

____

____

____

____

Why do you think these gadgets are essential to your life?

____

____

____

____

How could your life be different if you did not have access to these tools?

____

____

____

____

Create a list of the technological tools you will use less of in the future.

1.

2.

3.

4.

5.

What positive activities do you plan to engage in with the additional time you now have available? (Such as completing one's homework or one's chores.).

____

____

____

____

Activity 22: Assisting hand

Just so you understand

There are certain moments in life when the tasks you have to complete will become too lengthy for you to undertake alone. Regardless of whether you suffer from executive functioning issues, nobody can accomplish everything independently and never need assistance. Ask a trustworthy elder or classmate for help when work appears too difficult to complete for you. A reliable adult is someone you understand and who keeps your best interests at heart. A trusted adult might be your parent, a beloved teacher, a counselor, or even a buddy's parent.

Sixth grader Zach has always had academic difficulties. He was under the impression that he could not start tasks on time and finish them within the allotted time because he could not fully comprehend the requirements of the assignments.

Zach struggled with duties as well. He disliked that his parents would always remind him to complete his responsibilities like household chores. Zach realized he needed assistance. He spoke with his school counselor, who suggested he make a list of individuals who might assist him with the daily tasks he had to complete. Zach compiled a list of people he could turn to for help, both adults and peers. On Zach's list of resources was his mother, who helped him with arithmetic, and his buddy Tom, who helped him keep up with his scientific notes. And his grandmother, who helped him with household tasks. And his friend, Elizabeth, helped him edit his English papers.

Your task

In the fingertips of the hand seen below, add the name of a separate reliable adult (or peer).

You may use this "helping hand" to find five individuals who can assist you with the chores you require to be done. Describe all the aspects that each of these five persons may help you with within the following sections.

Name of a responsible person (or friend)

___

Topics and fields where this individual may assist me:

___

Name of a responsible person (or friend)

___

Topics and fields where this individual may assist me:

___

Name of a responsible person (or friend)

___

Topics and fields where this individual may assist me:

___

Name of a responsible person (or friend)

Topics and fields where this individual may assist me:

Name of a responsible person (or friend)

Topics and fields where this individual may assist me:

Added tasks

Write down three things you may need assistance with during the upcoming month.

1.
2.
3.

Before contacting someone on your list to ask for assistance when you need to do these chores, take the following procedures.

1. Give it your best shot before resorting to seeking assistance:
Only seek assistance after attempting to do the activity yourself.

2. Recognize your own need for assistance:

Although doing this might be challenging, nobody is counting on you to become an expert or to handle every task alone. Reassure yourself that asking for assistance is acceptable.

3. Specify the assistance you require:

Do what you can if you can only do a portion of the assignment and need help with the other parts.

4. Find the right individual to assist:

Your mother can help you with arithmetic, but not chemistry.

You wouldn't get assistance from your instructor to bathe your doggy. Make sure to locate the best person to assist you with your needs.

Having the courage to seek assistance from others can be challenging. However, if you ask them nicely, most people will happily lend you a hand. Make an effort to behave well whenever you are getting assistance. Pay attention to make the other person feel useful; if you succeed in doing so, they may feel more willing to assist you in the future if you make a similar request.

Finally, remember the important takeaway. Pay attention to how the person is assisting you, and make a mental note of what they are telling you so that the next time you have to do the same work on your own, you will have the abilities necessary to do so successfully.

Activity 23: Procrastination Issues

Just so you know

Pushing off a job you'd prefer not to complete is known as procrastination. Kids with poor executive functioning often put off dull tasks by telling themselves they'll do them afterward and decide to engage in something enjoyable instead. Although if you manage to briefly divert yourself by doing something else you'd prefer to be doing, delaying the activity will make you feel more stressed about completing it and decrease the likelihood that you'll have enough time to accomplish it well.

The fifteen-year-old Scott usually struggled with beginning and finishing things at home. His parents often told him to "get moving" on his tasks. Rather than accomplishing what he ought to be doing, he always ended up finding something else to do.

Finally, Scott's father broached the subject of his procrastination at a family gathering. Scott said he disliked completing chores and assignments because he considered them "boring." After hearing what he had to say, his parents concluded that he should use the timer to help him determine how long he should spend on his schoolwork and chores. He would have completed his work for the day once the timer went off. One minute should be subtracted from the total time shown on the timer weekly.

Initially, Scott could not do the assignment before the alarm went off. When he fixed the timer, he found that it often failed to begin immediately. This insight led him to start his subsequent work as soon as he had set his timer. Shortly afterward, Scott developed the habit of reliably finishing his chores and school assignments before the alarm sounded. After he became aware of how many hours he was squandering, Scott discovered that he might have more time to accomplish the things he wanted to do as soon as his responsibilities, such as his schoolwork and housework, were completed.

Your tasks

Some procrastinators need more skills to begin a task. Some people put off doing something since they worry they won't succeed, will seem silly, or will be seen as incompetent by others.

Make a table and list the things you may put off in the first column by thinking about them. Describe why you do not want to undertake each activity in the second column.

Avoiding responsibilities	Arguments in favor of avoiding it
Cutting grass on the lawn	I don't know how to operate a lawnmower.

Added tasks

Procrastination often results in issues in your life.

Draw an image of a moment you put off a job in the frame after this one. Then respond to the associated questions.

Once I decide to procrastinate..

What was the situation?

What made you put this off?

What issues did this cause you to have?

How were you feeling?

Sketch a picture of a moment you completed a job without delay in the next frame. Then respond to the associated questions.

A moment when I decided I would go against procrastinating…

What was the situation?

Why didn't you opt to put this work off?

What favorable outcomes resulted from your accomplishment of this task?

How were you feeling?

Take a glance at the drawing you made. Which makes you feel more positive about yourself? (Circle the response.)

The initial **The following**

What else can you learn from the subsequent circumstance that will enable you to perform effectively during the first?

How would you alter your behavior in the circumstances similar to the first one to assist you in putting off tasks less often in the coming years?

Activity 24: Perspective is crucial

Just so you understand

Your point of view is how you see the world. Perspectives may shift, which is fortunate since some individuals have an optimistic outlook and "see the glass as half full," while others have a pessimistic attitude and "see the glass as half empty."

Greg, who was thirteen, had a grudge. He believed that the only reason his buddies wanted to spend time out with him was so Greg could help them with homework. Greg felt that his professors detested him; he thought his mom and dad were trying to ruin his life. Greg became enraged as a consequence. He would start conflicts with friends, disputes with his parents all the time, and wake up grumpy. Greg had, at long last, reached his breaking point. He went to talk to the guidance counselor at his school to find out whether or not there was anything she could do to stop others from bothering him.

The only person Greg could influence, according to her psychotherapist, was himself. She claimed that his cynicism and tendency to anticipate the worse from others influenced how he handled others, affecting how others treated him. At first, Greg had a hard time accepting it as accurate.

He invested a significant amount of time and effort into convincing his therapist that the other people in his life were the source of his misery. After several sessions, Greg reached a point where He began to consider the possibility that his counselor was correct. Instead of constantly searching for the problems, he tried to identify the positives in the situation. Greg began reevaluating his relationship with his close buddies. It turned out that his friends were interested in him not just because he was good with homework; instead, they enjoyed spending time with him. His mom and dad stopped fighting with him after Greg attempted to get along with them and complete his responsibilities. When he started doing homework, his professors were also happier. Once he altered his outlook and actions, others treated him differently, making Greg happy too.

Your tasks

Your point of view is like a set of colored glasses that color the world you perceive. Viewing individuals and circumstances in your lives in a "negative" light might make you somewhat more pessimistic.

Write two unfavorable perspectives concerning each of the following circumstances on the lines. You may put down negative ideas or forecasts. Then, consider how you would feel if you saw the event in this manner. On a scale ranging from one to five, where one is mild, and five is strong, write the name of a sensation and mark the intensity to which you believe you would experience it.

Condition 1

Your mother instructs you to clean the dishes when you come home after school.

____

_______ Feelings ___________: 1 2 3 4 5

Condition 2

Your instructor gives you a task that includes making a PowerPoint presentation and presenting it to the students in the class.

____

_______ Feelings ___________: 1 2 3 4 5

Condition 3

You have come to know from your dentist that you have a cavity.

____

_______ Feelings ___________: 1 2 3 4 5

Extra to do

Make a mental shift and think of two constructive ways to look at each scenario from the previous exercise to get a more optimistic outlook on the circumstances. If you saw the method from this perspective, how would you feel about it?

On a scale of one to five, where one is mild, and five is strong, write the name of a sensation and mark the intensity to which you believe you would experience it.

Condition 1

Your mother instructs you to clean the dishes when you leave school.

____

____________Feelings ____________: 1 2 3 4 5

Condition 2

Your instructor gives you a task that includes making a presentation and presenting it to the class.

____

____________Feelings ____________: 1 2 3 4 5

Condition 3

You have come to know from your dentist that you have a cavity.

____

____________Feelings ____________: 1 2 3 4 5

Now contrast your answers with those from the prior exercise. Did your negative emotion about the issue lessen in intensity or change into a pleasing sensation when your viewpoint was more optimistic?

Activity 25: Achieving victory over your "beast"

For your information

Many children not skilled in executive functioning begin to have unfavorable thoughts about themselves. Those people start to feel that their shortcomings make them less capable than other individuals because of this. By maintaining a wall between who you are as a person and your shortcomings, you will be better able to externalize the issue (i.e., detach it from yourself) and try to improve it without allowing it to have a detrimental effect on your personality.

It might be challenging to identify your areas of weakness. Even though you know where you need to improve, you may still feel there is no possibility of improvement. It would be best to focus on improving your executive abilities to become stronger at almost everything you perform. Taking a step back and assessing your position from an outside perspective is helpful. If you've figured out how to do this, even though it's not always easy to accomplish, you'll be much better at recognizing what aspects of a situation you can influence and which you can't. After that, you may start adjusting to your life to help it go on the right path.

What you need to do

The executive abilities that need the most significant development on my part are:	Something that I am still terrified of despite having overcome it in the past.
Illustration of beasts that comprises both mentioned above.	

Write down the executive abilities that require the most remarkable improvements in the first box of this table. Fill out the second box with the name of an actual beast that frightened you as a child or perhaps still now.

After filling in these columns, it's time to generate a photograph of a "beast" that stands mutually for your executive confines and the beast you fear.

Added tasks

It is easier to comprehend that you can take action to overcome or lessen the effect of your weakness when you think of it as a "beast" that sometimes appears rather than as a component of you or something inside of you.

Please share your thoughts on the "beast" you drew by answering the following questions.

In what manner does this creature wreak havoc on your life?

____

What satisfies this "beast"?

____

What kind of ruses does this "beast" utilize to achieve objectives?

____

What do you think of the havoc this "beast" creates?

____

What agitates this "beast"?

____

Can you do anything to stop this "beast" from devouring your life?

____

How can you ensure that this "beast" doesn't return?

____

To Whom can you contact for support if you need it to battle this "beast"?

____

Activity 26: Check your stance before you run

For your information

A choice between acting and not acting in a particular circumstance might have repercussions, referred to as consequences. Consequences may be beneficial at times but detrimental at other times. Children with problems controlling their impulses often only learn the negative repercussions of their acts.

When it comes to children who struggle with weaknesses in their executive functioning, it may be challenging to stop and consider the repercussions of a decision before acting on it. They cannot control themselves from engaging in behaviors they know might have adverse consequences.

Critically analyzing your activities' potential outcomes may be a very beneficial endeavor. If you make it a habit to swiftly consider the consequences of your actions before committing to one of them, you will grow more proficient at making choices that are in your best interests.

For you to do

Examining the potential outcomes of a course of action before simply carrying it out is essential to making sound judgments.

The following is a list of potential activities for you to do. Try to devise one good and one bad possible result for each action, and then write them down in the appropriate spaces. Even if you put in much effort, it's hard to come up with a good reason to do something that seems terrible (or a wrong reason to do something that appears acceptable). One of the benefits of winning concert tickets is that you may enjoy a night out without worrying about breaking the bank. On the other hand, the unfavorable effect could be that you ought to skip an enjoyable television program.

Activity: You go out and buy a ticket for the lottery.

Good consequence:

Adverse consequence:

Activity: You start your day off with some doughnuts.

Good consequence:

Adverse consequence:

Activity: You perform your tasks.

Good consequence:

Adverse consequence:

Activity: You only do some of your assigned assignments.

Good consequence:

Adverse consequence:

Activity: You engage in conversation with your buddies by telephone.

Good consequence:

Adverse consequence:

Activity: You speak up and say something to the class.

Good consequence:

Adverse consequence:

Activity: You argue with your mother and father.

Good consequence:

Adverse consequence:

Activity: You cut into someone else's talk.

Good consequence:

Bad consequence:

More to do

There are instances when the consequences of our actions do not instantly become clear. We may not know the outcome of a choice for a few days, a few months, or perhaps a few years. It is often more challenging to make sound choices when the results of those choices are not immediately apparent. For instance, as the detrimental effects of smoking on health don't appear immediately, a young person who starts smoking may think it's OK to do so. Consider some short-term and long-term repercussions of the following choices before you make them.

Judgment: Consumc junk food.

Instant concerns:

Long-term concerns:

Judgment: Waste time on video games.

Instant concerns:

Long-term concerns:

Judgment: Workout

Instant concerns:

Long-term concerns:

Judgment: Do my assigned assignment.

Immediate concerns:

Long-term concerns:

Make a list of the decisions you've made recently that may have lasting effects, and then go through the process again for each.

Judgment:

Instant consequences:

Long-term repercussions include:

Judgment:

Instant consequences:

Long-term repercussions include:

Judgment:

Instant consequences:

Long-term repercussions include:

Judgment:

Instant consequences:

Long-term repercussions include:

Judgment:

Instant consequences:

Long-term repercussions include:

Activity 27: Taking a stance against your contemporaries

For your information

Children must acquire the skills necessary to cope with the challenges presented by peer group pressure. It can load this transitional moment with risks for kids with a deficiency in behavior management. Children unable to maintain control over their actions are more prone to comply with the recommendations of their contemporaries, even if this may not always be to their best advantage.

Omar, who was just fourteen, had a large circle of acquaintances. During the weekends, he often visited their home to socialize with them. One Sunday, his buddy Bill urged him to light a cigarette. Since Omar did not want his buddies to think of him as "a baby," he decided to take the cigarette Bill offered him.

Tracy and her buddy Sue, aged fifteen, were window shopping together at a store selling apparel. Sue instructed Tracy to change into jeans and wear them underneath her sweatpants in the dressing room. Sue responded to Tracy's objection, saying, "Everybody takes stuff occasionally." Tracy continued to argue. Whom is it going to hurt?

Franklin, who was just twelve at the time, approached John and requested that he may copy his schoolwork. John expressed that he did not consider it a wise option, but Franklin persisted with him, insisting that nobody would discover the truth.

Much more to do

Although you have certainly not been forced to do anything, it's still an excellent impression to study how to respectfully decline invitations from friends while maintaining a positive self-image. This exercise will teach you how to do both.

Consider if any of your close friends have ever requested you to participate in an activity you were unwilling to perform. Fill out the following table with some of the activities your friends have tried to get you to do, even if you knew it wasn't the best choice.

The next step is to get some experience finding excuses not to do each activity.

Actions that your buddies have requested	**Why say "sorry."**
Rather than completing your schoolwork, you should play a video game.	I wish I could, but I must go home since my parents are waiting for me.

Activity 28: Flexibility

For your information

Learning how to be flexible is a precious talent. Relaxed people are considerably better at managing circumstances that did not go as planned. Yet, children who struggle with executive functioning issues often work with adaptability.

Stretch Armstrong was the name of a toy that was quite popular. Stretch Armstrong was a significant action figure with much wiggle room and could be pushed, twisted, or curved in various ways. The children might tie together even just the limbs and legs of Stretch. The term "flexibility" refers to the capacity of anything to be bent, molded, stretched, or otherwise shaped. Athletes, who put their muscles through a significant amount of motion, benefit significantly from having elasticity in their bodies. Warming up with stretching is common among athletes to reduce the risk of pulling a muscle. Yet, being flexible extends beyond one's physical capabilities.

Agility in many other areas, such as the mind and emotions, is also essential. Children who aren't psychologically or cognitively adaptable have a tough time transitioning from one task to the next, and they also need help adapting to unforeseen changes in their routines.

By exercise and practice, you may increase not just your physical flexibility but also your mental and emotional flexibility. You may develop more mental and emotional flexibility in the same way you develop physical flexibility.

Your tasks

You must follow the instructions for each component of the activity. To complete this activity, you will need pastels, marker pens, or colored pencils in the following hues: yellow, blue, orange, green, and red.

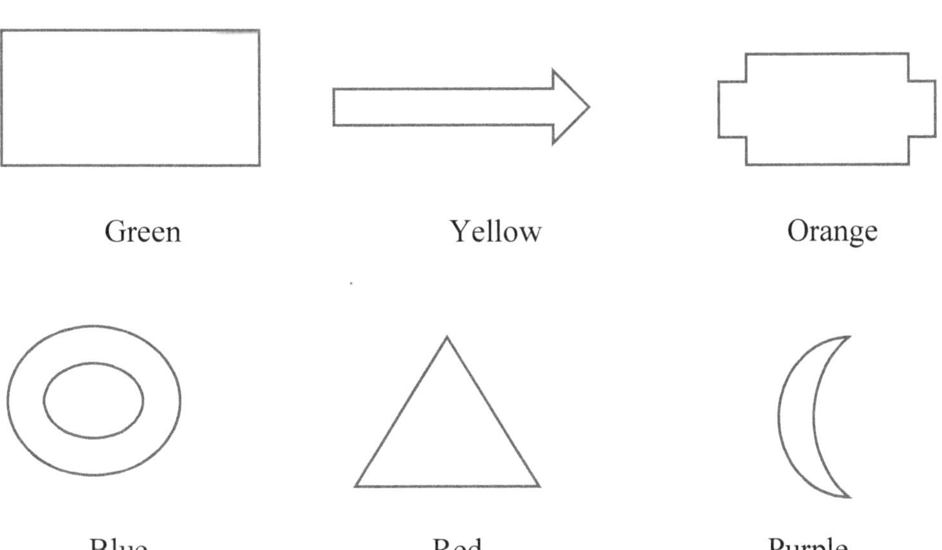

1. Give each of the shapes the color specified below it.

Blue

Purple

Green

Yellow

Orange

Red

2. Don't underline or highlight any of the following words.

Blue

Purple

Green

Yellow

Orange

Red

3. Please select a shade that is not given for each word underneath. Use any hue other than green to represent the word "green," for instance.

Blue

Purple

Green

Yellow

Orange

Red

More to do

Use a stopwatch or watch with a second hand to time you identifying all the forms' colors from part 1 of the preceding segment's activity.

____________ Time units

Next, time yourself reading the second section's text and record your results (which you did not color).

____________ Time units

The last stage is to record how long it takes you to recognize all of the colors of the words from part 3 (the colors you selected instead of what the phrases say), one at a time (repeat the process if necessary).

____________ Time units

Time yourself again as you spend one minute identifying the colors in the third portion of the exercise.

____________ Time units

Did you notice a reduction in your time? (Please circle your response.)

No **Yes**

Why do you believe this to be the case?

___

How can participating in this exercise help you better comprehend the mental flexibility you possess?

___

Activity 29: Improvising

For your information

Children having difficulty with activities demanding executive abilities often have less cognitive flexibility than their classmates. Improvisational practice is one technique to develop the mental flexibility you already possess.

When you improvise, you find a resourceful answer to a problem that uses whatever is at hand, regardless of whether or not those are the most effective options for the task.

Improvisation is innovative problem-solving. It often calls for using one's imagination, a potent instrument.

Whenever we improvise, we sometimes create a tale to accompany the circumstance. This improvisation is recommended for actors who wish to enhance their acting talents. Improvisation may sometimes take the form of parents telling bedtime stories to their children that they make up as they go along. Below is one example. You've probably done improvisation if you've had to think of a solution to an issue that may be devised "on the move." To be resourceful, or to improvise, might imply finding an unanticipated use for something or utilizing something in a new way. You may use tongs to reach an item on a high shelf in your kitchen without using a chair or step stool. It would be an instance of becoming industrious.

You have something to do

List as many inventive (i.e., non-standard) applications as possible for each of the following things. For instance, the leading one has already been completed for you.

Safety Pin

When used typically: To bind cloth together

Innovative applications: To open envelopes, as earrings, to hold documents together, to eliminate splinters, and to poke tiny holes.

Fork

When used typically: to eat

Innovative uses:

Pillow

When used typically: To relax or sleep

Innovative applications:

Hammer

When used typically: To drive nails into boards by pounding.

Innovative applications:

Toothbrush

When used typically: To keep your teeth clean

Innovative applications:

Bandage

The typical use is to conceal wounds.

Innovative applications:

Much more to do

Things that are not well-planned in your daily life will occur in your life. When something like this occurs, it is helpful if you are prepared to "go with the flow."

Write down what you would do if you had to improvise in every one of the following scenarios and explain how you would accomplish it. As an illustration, the leading one has already been completed for you.

Situation:

You have an anniversary celebration planned, but your mother only bought enough food for six people even though ten people will turn up.
Example:

Please suggest a meal that she can prepare in a short amount of time that will feed all people.

Situation:

Your mom called to tell you that your relatives were arriving for supper, so you had to head home immediately. In contrast, you and a friend planned to stay at the mall.

Situation:

Your math instructor has just informed you that there will be a surprise exam tomorrow. You still need to do revision to prepare for this exam.

Situation:

As you provide food for your pet, the bottle's lid suddenly falls off. Food is everywhere on the ground, and your mother will be home after a few minutes.

Situation:

You get a text message from a buddy inviting you to watch a movie when you are in the middle of cleaning your room.

Situation:

You have about half an hour to prepare before reporting to your new tuition, but your clothes are filthy.

Situation:

You are using the computer to work on a history assignment for school when suddenly the electricity goes out. Your work has not been saved.

Activity 30: I need it broken down!

For your information

When someone faces a challenge that looks insurmountable, it's natural to feel hesitant about taking it on. It's possible to make nearly any job more doable by dividing it into smaller, highly manageable chunks, even if the whole thing initially appears overwhelming.

Daphne, who was in sixth grade, would put off doing her school assignments until the very last minute. Then, to complete the task as quickly as possible, she would speed through it and do a lousy job.

The next stage was for daphne and her mother to put their thoughts down on paper as step-by-step instructions for the project. Now, daphne has a written list of instructions for every step of the process and a deadline for when she will finish it. Daphne's perception of the project improved as a result, and she could unwind more easily since she was no longer under the impression that she needed to do the whole thing at once.

When daphne handed in her physics task, she acknowledged a grade far higher than she had previously received for hastily completed tasks. She was pleased with her achievement, and in the days to come, she applied the same methodology to all her schoolwork assignments.

You have something to do

The following are the project instructions Daphne's physics instructor wrote down for the class.

Select a creature you like from the realm of the animals. Create an attractive picture of the animals and correctly name their genus, class, order, phylum, family, and species. The "ordinary" name of the animals must come first on the list. The deadline for this project is the fifteen of March.

The process of completing the project was broken down into the following phases by Daphne and her mother. Mark them from one to seven by the sequence wherein you believe they should be completed, and then provide an appropriate deadline for each. Remember that some of the stages will take much more time than others. (Suppose she handed out the assignment on the first of March.)

Much more to do

The first step is determining what project phases are required to break it down.

The first step is often the most crucial but may also be the most challenging.

Try to work out the first step you must take to get started with every one of the following tasks. The next step is to consult with some friends or your parents to determine the initial move, then contrast their thoughts to yours. Are things going in the correct direction for you? As an illustration, the leading one has already been completed for you.

Portrait a Bedroom

Step 1: Consider the hues available to you before making a decision.

Taking Care of Your cupboard

Step 1:

Doing Maths Assignments

Step 1:

Giving a bath to a cat

Step 1:

Creating a Report on a Book

Step 1:

Washing the kitchen dishes

Step 1:

Writing a Historical Project

Step 1:

Conclusion

Like other developmental milestones, the rate at which children succeed in executive function varies according to the child. Some children have more significant delays or setbacks in maturing their capacity for the organizational process. Yet, less confident children have difficulties or delays greater than usual concerning their administrative function abilities.

In some children, difficulties in executive function manifest themselves as problems with impulse control, outbursts of anger, and a lack of ability to self-regulate their emotions. Others need help with schoolwork, managing their time effectively, and recalling instructions when they have difficulties. Teenagers who have trouble with executive function frequently experience a hard time becoming independent and coming up with future strategies.

Executive functioning difficulties are a problem for many children, particularly those with attention deficit hyperactivity disorder (ADHD), intellectual impairments, average intelligence autism, or several other issues. This workbook provides these children (and their families) with techniques to strengthen their executive functions, which indicates that they may build abilities that will improve the quality of their lives.

This book will be an excellent resource for people of all ages, including students, teachers, and parents. As a counselor for years, I am confident that you will find this resource beneficial in assisting your children in achieving success in executive functioning!

It will serve as a beneficial instrument for executive abilities, trainers, and professors responsible for creating organizational skills seminars for students in their classes.

These workbook exercises and activities are flexible enough to be utilized by individual children or pupils in groups. Furthermore, mentors and workshop representatives can easily select which executive abilities to emphasize and which activities to implement due to the tasks' and exercises' adaptability.

Resources

Miller, A. L., Lee, H. J., & Lumeng, J. C. (2015). Obesity-associated biomarkers and executive function in children. *Pediatric research, 77*(1), 143-147.

Dovis, S., Van der Oord, S., Wiers, R. W., & Prins, P. J. (2015). Improving executive functioning in children with ADHD: training multiple executive functions within the context of a computer game. A randomized double-blind placebo controlled trial. *PloS one, 10*(4), e0121651.

Lai, C. L. E., Lau, Z., Lui, S. S., Lok, E., Tam, V., Chan, Q., ... & Cheung, E. F. (2017). Meta-analysis of neuropsychological measures of executive functioning in children and adolescents with high-functioning autism spectrum disorder. *Autism Research, 10*(5), 911-939.

Cohen, J. F., Gorski, M. T., Gruber, S. A., Kurdziel, L. B. F., & Rimm, E. B. (2016). The effect of healthy dietary consumption on executive cognitive functioning in children and adolescents: a systematic review. *British Journal of Nutrition, 116*(6), 989-1000.

Doebel, S., & Zelazo, P. D. (2015). A meta-analysis of the Dimensional Change Card Sort: Implications for developmental theories and the measurement of executive function in children. *Developmental Review, 38*, 241-268.

Pauls, L. J., & Archibald, L. M. (2016). Executive functions in children with specific language impairment: A meta-analysis. *Journal of speech, language, and hearing research, 59*(5), 1074-1086.

Barbosa, T., Rodrigues, C. C., Mello, C. B. D., & Bueno, O. F. A. (2019). Executive functions in children with dyslexia. *Arquivos de Neuro-psiquiatria, 77*, 254-259.

Doebel, S. (2020). Rethinking executive function and its development. *Perspectives on Psychological Science, 15*(4), 942-956.

Mak, C., Whittingham, K., Cunnington, R., & Boyd, R. N. (2018). Efficacy of mindfulness-based interventions for attention and executive function in children and adolescents—A systematic review. *Mindfulness, 9*, 59-78.

Purpura, D. J., Schmitt, S. A., & Ganley, C. M. (2017). Foundations of mathematics and literacy: The role of executive functioning components. *Journal of experimental child psychology, 153*, 15-34.